MznLnx

Missing Links Exam Preps

Exam Prep for

Applied Calculus for Business, Economics, Life Sciences, and Social Sciences

Barnett, Ziegler, Byleen, 7th Edition

The MznLnx Exam Prep is your link from the texbook and lecture to your exams.
The MznLnx Exam Preps are unauthorized and comprehensive reviews of your textbooks.

All material provided by MznLnx and Rico Publications (c) 2010
Textbook publishers and textbook authors do not particpate in or contribute to these reviews.

MznLnx

Rico Publications

Exam Prep for Applied Calculus for Business, Economics, Life Sciences, and Social Sciences
7th Edition
Barnett, Ziegler, Byleen

Publisher: Raymond Houge
Assistant Editor: Michael Rouger
Text and Cover Designer: Lisa Buckner
Marketing Manager: Sara Swagger
Project Manager, Editorial Production: Jerry Emerson
Art Director: Vernon Lowerui

Product Manager: Dave Mason
Editorial Assitant: Rachel Guzmanji
Pedagogy: Debra Long
Cover Image: Jim Reed/Getty Images
Text and Cover Printer: City Printing, Inc.
Compositor: Media Mix, Inc.

(c) 2010 Rico Publications

ALL RIGHTS RESERVED. No part of this work covered by the copyright may be reproduced or used in any form or by an means--graphic, electronic, or mechanical, including photocopying, recording, taping, Web distribution, information storage, and retrieval systems, or in any other manner--without the written permission of the publisher.

Printed in the United States
ISBN:

For more information about our products, contact us at:

Dave.Mason@RicoPublications.com

For permission to use material from this text or

product, submit a request online to:

Dave.Mason@RicoPublications.com

Contents

CHAPTER 1
A Beginning Library of Elementary Functions ... 1

CHAPTER 2
Additional Elementary Functions ... 15

CHAPTER 3
The Derivative ... 28

CHAPTER 4
Graphing and Optimization ... 42

CHAPTER 5
Additional Derivative Topics ... 57

CHAPTER 6
Integration ... 70

CHAPTER 7
Additional Integration Topics ... 86

CHAPTER 8
Multivariable Calculus ... 96

CHAPTER 9
Differential Equations ... 111

CHAPTER 10
Taylor Polynomials and Infinite Series ... 121

CHAPTER 11
Probability and Calculus ... 125

CHAPTER 12
Trigonometric Functions ... 131

ANSWER KEY ... 135

TO THE STUDENT

COMPREHENSIVE

The *MznLnx* Exam Prep series is designed to help you pass your exams. Editors at MznLnx review your textbooks and then prepare these practice exams to help you master the textbook material. Unlike study guides, workbooks, and practice tests provided by the texbook publisher and textbook authors, *MznLnx* gives you **all** of the material in each chapter in exam form, not just samples, so you can be sure to nail your exam.

MECHANICAL

The MznLnx Exam Prep series creates exams that will help you learn the subject matter as well as test you on your understanding. Each question is designed to help you master the concept. Just working through the exams, you gain an understanding of the subject--its a simple mechanical process that produces success.

INTEGRATED STUDY GUIDE AND REVIEW

MznLnx is not just a set of exams designed to test you, its also a comprehensive review of the subject content. Each exam question is also a review of the concept, making sure that you will get the answer correct without having to go to other sources of material. You learn as you go! Its the easiest way to pass an exam.

HUMOR

Studying can be tedious and dry. MznLnx's instructional design includes moderate humor within the exam questions on occassion, to break the tedium and revitalize the brain

Chapter 1. A Beginning Library of Elementary Functions 1

1. In mathematics, a _____ in elementary terms is any of a variety of different functions from geometry, such as rotations, reflections and translations.
   a. Thing
   b. Transformation0
   c. Undefined
   d. Undefined

2. A _____ is a polynomial function of the form f(x) = ax^2 + bx +c , where a, b, c are real numbers and a , 0.
   a. Quadratic function0
   b. Event
   c. Undefined
   d. Undefined

3. _____ are the basic objects of study in graph theory. Informally speaking, a graph is a set of objects called points, nodes, or vertices connected by links called lines or edges.
   a. Graphs0
   b. Thing
   c. Undefined
   d. Undefined

4. _____ are objects, characters, or other concrete representations of ideas, concepts, or other abstractions.
   a. Thing
   b. Symbols0
   c. Undefined
   d. Undefined

5. The word _____ comes from the Latin word linearis, which means created by lines.
   a. Linear0
   b. Thing
   c. Undefined
   d. Undefined

6. A _____ is a first degree polynomial mathematical function of the form: f(x) = mx + b where m and b are real constants and x is a real variable.
   a. Thing
   b. Linear function0
   c. Undefined
   d. Undefined

7. The mathematical concept of a _____ expresses the intuitive idea of deterministic dependence between two quantities, one of which is viewed as primary and the other as secondary. A _____ then is a way to associate a unique output for each input of a specified type, for example, a real number or an element of a given set.
   a. Function0
   b. Thing
   c. Undefined
   d. Undefined

8. A _____ is a set of numbers that designate location in a given reference system, such as x,y in a planar _____ system or an x,y,z in a three-dimensional _____ system.
   a. Thing
   b. Coordinate0
   c. Undefined
   d. Undefined

9. In mathematics and its applications, a _____ is a system for assigning an n-tuple of numbers or scalars to each point in an n-dimensional space.
   a. Coordinate system0
   b. Concept
   c. Undefined
   d. Undefined

10. Mathematical _____ is used to represent ideas.
    a. Notation0
    b. Thing
    c. Undefined
    d. Undefined

Chapter 1. A Beginning Library of Elementary Functions

11. In mathematics, a _____ is a two-dimensional manifold or surface that is perfectly flat.
    a. Thing
    b. Plane0
    c. Undefined
    d. Undefined

12. _____ means of or relating to the French philosopher and mathematician René Descartes.
    a. Cartesian0
    b. Thing
    c. Undefined
    d. Undefined

13. In mathematics, the _____ is used to determine each point uniquely in a plane through two numbers, usually called the x-coordinate and the y-coordinate of the point.
    a. Cartesian coordinate system0
    b. Thing
    c. Undefined
    d. Undefined

14. An _____ is a straight line around which a geometric figure can be rotated.
    a. Thing
    b. Axis0
    c. Undefined
    d. Undefined

15. In astronomy, geography, geometry and related sciences and contexts, a plane is said to be _____ at a given point if it is locally perpendicular to the gradient of the gravity field, i.e., with the direction of the gravitational force at that point.
    a. Thing
    b. Horizontal0
    c. Undefined
    d. Undefined

16. A _____ consists of one quarter of the coordinate plane.
    a. Quadrant0
    b. Thing
    c. Undefined
    d. Undefined

17. An _____ is when two lines intersect somewhere on a plane creating a right angle at intersection
    a. Thing
    b. Axes0
    c. Undefined
    d. Undefined

18. The _____ is the y- coordinate of a point within a two dimensional coordinate system. It is sometimes used to refer to the axis rather than the distance along the coordinate system.
    a. Thing
    b. Ordinate0
    c. Undefined
    d. Undefined

19. In mathematics, the _____ of a coordinate system is the point where the axes of the system intersect.
    a. Thing
    b. Origin0
    c. Undefined
    d. Undefined

20. _____ consists of the first element in a coordinate pair. When graphed in the coordinate plane, it is the distance from the y-axis. Frequently called the x coordinate.
    a. Thing
    b. Abscissa0
    c. Undefined
    d. Undefined

21. In mathematics, a _____ may be described informally as a number that can be given by an infinite decimal representation.

a. Real number0
b. Thing
c. Undefined
d. Undefined

22. An _____ is a collection of two not necessarily distinct objects, one of which is distinguished as the first coordinate and the other as the second coordinate.
   a. Ordered pair0
   b. Thing
   c. Undefined
   d. Undefined

23. _____ is the study of geometry using the principles of algebra. _____ can be explained more simply: it is concerned with defining geometrical shapes in a numerical way and extracting numerical information from that representation.
   a. Analytic geometry0
   b. Thing
   c. Undefined
   d. Undefined

24. In mathematics, a _____ is a statement that can be proved on the basis of explicitly stated or previously agreed assumptions.
   a. Theorem0
   b. Thing
   c. Undefined
   d. Undefined

25. In number theory, the _____ of arithmetic (or unique factorization theorem) states that every natural number greater than 1 can be written as a unique product of prime numbers.
   a. Concept
   b. Fundamental theorem0
   c. Undefined
   d. Undefined

26. An _____ or member of a set is an object that when collected together make up the set.
   a. Element0
   b. Thing
   c. Undefined
   d. Undefined

27. In mathematics, the _____ , or members of a set or more generally a class are all those objects which when collected together make up the set or class.
   a. Thing
   b. Elements0
   c. Undefined
   d. Undefined

28. A _____ is a set of possible values that a variable can take on in order to satisfy a given set of conditions, which may include equations and inequalities.
   a. Thing
   b. Solution set0
   c. Undefined
   d. Undefined

29. _____ is the state of being greater than any finite real or natural number, however large.
   a. Thing
   b. Infinite0
   c. Undefined
   d. Undefined

30. In mathematics, the conjugate _____ or adjoint matrix of an m-by-n matrix A with complex entries is the n-by-m matrix A* obtained from A by taking the transpose and then taking the complex conjugate of each entry.

a. Thing   b. Pairs0
c. Undefined   d. Undefined

31. In mathematics, the concept of a _____ tries to capture the intuitive idea of a geometrical one-dimensional and continuous object. A simple example is the circle.
a. Thing   b. Curve0
c. Undefined   d. Undefined

32. In mathematics, the _____ is a conic section generated by the intersection of a right circular conical surface and a plane parallel to a generating straight line of that surface. It can also be defined as locus of points in a plane which are equidistant from a given point.
a. Parabola0   b. Thing
c. Undefined   d. Undefined

33. In mathematics, an _____, mean, or central tendency of a data set refers to a measure of the "middle" or "expected" value of the data set.
a. Average0   b. Concept
c. Undefined   d. Undefined

34. _____ is a physical property of a system that underlies the common notions of hot and cold; something that is hotter has the greater _____.
a. Temperature0   b. Thing
c. Undefined   d. Undefined

35. A _____ is a statement or claimt that a particular event will occur in the future in more certain terms than a forecast.
a. Prediction0   b. Thing
c. Undefined   d. Undefined

36. _____ is the application of tools and a processing medium to the transformation of raw materials into finished goods for sale.
a. Manufacturing0   b. Thing
c. Undefined   d. Undefined

37. In mathematics, the _____ of a function is the set of all "output" values produced by that function. Given a function $f : A \to B$, the _____ of f, is defined to be the set $\{x \in B : x = f(a)$ for some $a \in A\}$.
a. Thing   b. Range0
c. Undefined   d. Undefined

38. In mathematics, a _____ of a k-place relation $L \subseteq X_1 \times \ldots \times X_k$ is one of the sets X_j, $1 \leq j \leq k$. In the special case where k = 2 and $L \subseteq X_1 \times X_2$ is a function $L : X_1 \to X_2$, it is conventional to refer to X_1 as the _____ of the function and to refer to X_2 as the codomain of the function.
a. Thing   b. Domain0
c. Undefined   d. Undefined

Chapter 1. A Beginning Library of Elementary Functions

39. A _____ is a symbolic representation denoting a quantity or expression. It often represents an "unknown" quantity that has the potential to change.
    a. Thing
    b. Variable0
    c. Undefined
    d. Undefined

40. In mathematics, an _____ is any of the arguments, i.e. "inputs", to a function. Thus if we have a function f(x), then x is a _____.
    a. Independent variable0
    b. Thing
    c. Undefined
    d. Undefined

41. In a function the _____, is the variable which is the value, i.e. the "output", of the function.
    a. Dependent variable0
    b. Thing
    c. Undefined
    d. Undefined

42. In plane geometry, a _____ is a polygon with four equal sides, four right angles, and parallel opposite sides. In algebra, the _____ of a number is that number multiplied by itself.
    a. Thing
    b. Square0
    c. Undefined
    d. Undefined

43. In mathematics, a _____ of a number x is a number r such that $r^2 = x$, or in words, a number r whose square (the result of multiplying the number by itself) is x.
    a. Square root0
    b. Thing
    c. Undefined
    d. Undefined

44. In mathematics, a _____ of a complex-valued function f is a member x of the domain of f such that f(x) vanishes at x, that is, x : f (x) = 0.
    a. Thing
    b. Root0
    c. Undefined
    d. Undefined

45. In mathematics, an inequality is a statement about the relative size or order of two objects. For example 14 > 10, or 14 is _____ 10.
    a. Thing
    b. Greater than0
    c. Undefined
    d. Undefined

46. In mathematics, an _____ is a statement about the relative size or order of two objects.
    a. Thing
    b. Inequality0
    c. Undefined
    d. Undefined

47. In elementary algebra, an _____ is a set that contains every real number between two indicated numbers and may contain the two numbers themselves.
    a. Thing
    b. Interval0
    c. Undefined
    d. Undefined

48. _____ is the notation in which permitted values for a variable are expressed as ranging over a certain interval; "5 < x < 9" is an example of the application of _____.

a. Thing
b. Interval notation0
c. Undefined
d. Undefined

49. In mathematics, a _____ is the result of multiplying, or an expression that identifies factors to be multiplied.
a. Product0
b. Thing
c. Undefined
d. Undefined

50. An _____ is a combination of numbers, operators, grouping symbols and/or free variables and bound variables arranged in a meaningful way which can be evaluated..
a. Expression0
b. Thing
c. Undefined
d. Undefined

51. _____, from Latin meaning "to make progress", is defined in two different ways. Pure economic _____ is the increase in wealth that an investor has from making an investment, taking into consideration all costs associated with that investment including the opportunity cost of capital.
a. Profit0
b. Thing
c. Undefined
d. Undefined

52. _____ is a synonym for information.
a. Thing
b. Data0
c. Undefined
d. Undefined

53. _____ is the part of statistical practice concerned with the selection of individual observations intended to yield some knowledge about a population of concern, especially for the purposes of statistical inference.
a. Thing
b. Sampling0
c. Undefined
d. Undefined

54. In economics, supply and _____ describe market relations between prospective sellers and buyers of a good.
a. Thing
b. Demand0
c. Undefined
d. Undefined

55. _____ is a business term for the amount of money that a company receives from its activities in a given period, mostly from sales of products and/or services to customers
a. Revenue0
b. Thing
c. Undefined
d. Undefined

56. According to the United Nations Statistics Division, _____ is the resale sale without transformation of new and used goods to retailers, to industrial, commercial, institutional or professional users, or to other wholesalers, or involves acting as an agent or broker in buying merchandise for, or selling merchandise, to such persons or companies.
a. Wholesale0
b. Thing
c. Undefined
d. Undefined

57. In common philosophical language, a proposition or _____, is the content of an assertion, that is, it is true-or-false and defined by the meaning of a particular piece of language.

Chapter 1. A Beginning Library of Elementary Functions 7

a. Statement0
b. Concept
c. Undefined
d. Undefined

58. A _____ is a three-dimensional solid object bounded by six square faces, facets, or sides, with three meeting at each vertex.
    a. Thing
    b. Cube0
    c. Undefined
    d. Undefined

59. _____ is the distance around a given two-dimensional object. As a general rule, the _____ of a polygon can always be calculated by adding all the length of the sides together. So, the formula for triangles is P = a + b + c, where a, b and c stand for each side of it. For quadrilaterals the equation is P = a + b + c + d. For equilateral polygons, P = na, where n is the number of sides and a is the side length.
    a. Perimeter0
    b. Thing
    c. Undefined
    d. Undefined

60. In geometry, a _____ is defined as a quadrilateral where all four of its angles are right angles.
    a. Thing
    b. Rectangle0
    c. Undefined
    d. Undefined

61. The _____ of measurement are a globally standardized and modernized form of the metric system.
    a. Units0
    b. Thing
    c. Undefined
    d. Undefined

62. A _____ is a function that assigns a number to subsets of a given set.
    a. Measure0
    b. Thing
    c. Undefined
    d. Undefined

63. The _____ of a solid object is the three-dimensional concept of how much space it occupies, often quantified numerically.
    a. Volume0
    b. Thing
    c. Undefined
    d. Undefined

64. In mathematics and the mathematical sciences, a _____ is a fixed, but possibly unspecified, value. This is in contrast to a variable, which is not fixed.
    a. Constant0
    b. Thing
    c. Undefined
    d. Undefined

65. _____ is a way of expressing a number as a fraction of 100 per cent meaning "per hundred".
    a. Percent0
    b. Thing
    c. Undefined
    d. Undefined

66. In Euclidean geometry, a _____ is moving every point a constant distance in a specified direction.
    a. Translation0
    b. Concept
    c. Undefined
    d. Undefined

67. A _____ is a number that is less than zero.

Chapter 1. A Beginning Library of Elementary Functions

    a. Negative number0   b. Thing
    c. Undefined   d. Undefined

68. In mathematics, a _____ (also spelled reflexion) is a map that transforms an object into its mirror image.
    a. Concept   b. Reflection0
    c. Undefined   d. Undefined

69. In combinatorial mathematics, a _____ is an un-ordered collection of unique elements.
    a. Combination0   b. Concept
    c. Undefined   d. Undefined

70. An _____ of a product of sums expresses it as a sum of products by using the fact that multiplication distributes over addition.
    a. Expansion0   b. Thing
    c. Undefined   d. Undefined

71. In a mathematical proof or a syllogism, a _____ is a statement that is the logical consequence of preceding statements.
    a. Concept   b. Conclusion0
    c. Undefined   d. Undefined

72. In mathematics, the _____ (or modulus) of a real number is its numerical value without regard to its sign.
    a. Thing   b. Absolute value0
    c. Undefined   d. Undefined

73. A _____ defined function $f(x)$ of a real variable x is a function whose definition is given differently on disjoint subsets of its domain.
    a. Piecewise0   b. Thing
    c. Undefined   d. Undefined

74. Order theory is a branch of mathematics that studies various kinds of binary relations that capture the intuitive notion of a mathematical _____.
    a. Thing   b. Ordering0
    c. Undefined   d. Undefined

75. The _____ integers are all the integers from zero on upwards.
    a. Nonnegative0   b. Thing
    c. Undefined   d. Undefined

76. An _____ is an equality that remains true regardless of the values of any variables that appear within it, to distinguish it from an equality which is true under more particular conditions.
    a. Thing   b. Identity0
    c. Undefined   d. Undefined

77. An _____ is a function that does not have any effect: it always returns the same value that was used as its argument.

Chapter 1. A Beginning Library of Elementary Functions

a. Identity function0
c. Undefined
b. Thing
d. Undefined

78. The word _____ is used in a variety of ways in mathematics.
   a. Index0
   c. Undefined
   b. Thing
   d. Undefined

79. A _____ is a negotiable instrument instructing a financial institution to pay a specific amount of a specific currency from a specific demand account held in the maker/depositor's name with that institution. Both the maker and payee may be natural persons or legal entities.
   a. Thing
   c. Undefined
   b. Check0
   d. Undefined

80. In mathematics, a _____ is an ordered list of objects. Like a set, it contains members, also called elements or terms, and the number of terms is called the length of the _____. Unlike a set, order matters, and the exact same elements can appear multiple times at different positions in the _____.
   a. Sequence0
   c. Undefined
   b. Thing
   d. Undefined

81. Continuous functions are of utmost importance in mathematics and applications. However, not all functions are continuous. If a function is not continuous at a point in its domain, one says that it has a _____ there. The set of all points of _____ of a function may be a discrete set, a dense set, or even the entire domain of the function.
   a. Thing
   c. Undefined
   b. Discontinuity0
   d. Undefined

82. In finance and economics, _____ is the process of finding the present value of an amount of cash at some future date, and along with compounding cash forms the basis of time value of money calculations.
   a. Discount0
   c. Undefined
   b. Thing
   d. Undefined

83. A _____ is a unit of length, usually used to measure distance, in a number of different systems, including Imperial units, United States customary units and Norwegian/Swedish mil. Its size can vary from system to system, but in each is between 1 and 10 kilometers. In contemporary English contexts _____ refers to either:
   a. Mile0
   c. Undefined
   b. Thing
   d. Undefined

84. In business, particularly accounting, a _____ is the time intervals that the accounts, statement, payments, or other calculations cover.
   a. Thing
   c. Undefined
   b. Period0
   d. Undefined

85. The process of sending accounts to customers for goods or services is called _____.
   a. Billing0
   c. Undefined
   b. Thing
   d. Undefined

86. The metre (or _____, see spelling differences) is a measure of length. It is the basic unit of length in the metric system and in the International System of Units (SI), used around the world for general and scientific purposes.
   a. Meter0
   b. Concept
   c. Undefined
   d. Undefined

87. _____ is a unit of speed, expressing the number of international miles covered per hour.
   a. Miles per hour0
   b. Thing
   c. Undefined
   d. Undefined

88. Any point where a graph makes contact with an coordinate axis is called an _____ of the graph
   a. Intercept0
   b. Thing
   c. Undefined
   d. Undefined

89. In mathematics, the _____ f is the collection of all ordered pairs . In particular, graph means the graphical representation of this collection, in the form of a curve or surface, together with axes, etc. Graphing on a Cartesian plane is sometimes referred to as curve sketching.
   a. Graph of a function0
   b. Thing
   c. Undefined
   d. Undefined

90. _____ is a function whose values do not vary and thus are constant.
   a. Thing
   b. Constant function0
   c. Undefined
   d. Undefined

91. In mathematics, a _____ is an expression that is constructed from one or more variables and constants, using only the operations of addition, subtraction, multiplication, and constant positive whole number exponents. is a _____. Note in particular that division by an expression containing a variable is not in general allowed in polynomials. [1]
   a. Thing
   b. Polynomial0
   c. Undefined
   d. Undefined

92. In linear algebra, the _____ of an n-by-n square matrix A is defined to be the sum of the elements on the main diagonal of A,
   a. Thing
   b. Trace0
   c. Undefined
   d. Undefined

93. A _____ is a tool similar to a ruler, but without markings.
   a. Thing
   b. Straightedge0
   c. Undefined
   d. Undefined

94. A _____ is a quantity that denotes the proportional amount or magnitude of one quantity relative to another.
   a. Ratio0
   b. Thing
   c. Undefined
   d. Undefined

95. _____ is often used to describe the measurement of the steepness, incline, gradient, or grade of a straight line. The _____ is defined as the ratio of the "rise" divided by the "run" between two points on a line, or in other words, the ratio of the altitude change to the horizontal distance between any two points on the line.

Chapter 1. A Beginning Library of Elementary Functions

a. Slope0
b. Thing
c. Undefined
d. Undefined

96. Fixed costs are expenses whose total does not change in proportion to the activity of a business.Unit fixed costs decline with volume following a retangular hyperbola as the volume of production.Variable costs by contrast change in relation to the activity of a business such as sales or production volume.Along with variable costs,fixed costs make up one of the two components of total cost. In the most simple production function total cost is equal to fixed costs plus variable costs.In accounting terminology, fixed costs will broadly include all costs which are not included in cost of goods sold, and variable costs are those captured in costs of goods sold. The implicit assumption required to make the equivalence between the accounting and economics terminology is that the accounting period is equal to the period in which fixed costs do not vary in relation to production. In practice, this equivalence does not always hold and depending on the period under consideration by management, some overhead expenses can be adjusted by management, and the specific allocation of each expense to each category will be decided under cost accounting.In business planning and management accounting, usage of the terms fixed costs, variable costs and others will often differ from usage in economics, and may depend on the intended use. For example, costs may be segregated into per unit costs fixed costs per period, and variable costs as a proportion of revenue. Capital expenditures will usually be allocated separately, and depending on the purpose, a portion may be regularly allocated to expenses as depreciation and amortization and seen as a _____ per period, or the entire amount may be considered upfront fixed costs.
a. Thing
b. Fixed cost0
c. Undefined
d. Undefined

97. _____ are expenses whose total does not change in proportion to the activity of a business, within the relevant time period or scale of production
a. Fixed costs0
b. Thing
c. Undefined
d. Undefined

98. _____, in law and economics, is a form of risk management primarily used to hedge against the risk of a contingent loss.
a. Insurance0
b. Thing
c. Undefined
d. Undefined

99. _____ is the fee paid on borrowed money.
a. Thing
b. Interest0
c. Undeflned
d. Undefined

100. _____ has many meanings, most of which simply .
a. Thing
b. Power0
c. Undefined
d. Undefined

101. _____ is a term used in accounting, economics and finance with reference to the fact that assets with finite lives lose value over time.
a. Thing
b. Depreciation0
c. Undefined
d. Undefined

102. A _____ is an equation in which each term is either a constant or the product of a constant times the first power of a variable.

a. Linear equation0
b. Thing
c. Undefined
d. Undefined

103. A _____ is an abstract model that uses mathematical language to describe the behavior of a system. Eykhoff defined a _____ as 'a representation of the essential aspects of an existing system which presents knowledge of that system in usable form'.
   a. Mathematical model0
   b. Thing
   c. Undefined
   d. Undefined

104. In the scientific method, an _____ (Latin: ex-+-periri, "of (or from) trying"), is a set of actions and observations, performed in the context of solving a particular problem or question, in order to support or falsify a hypothesis or research concerning phenomena.
   a. Experiment0
   b. Thing
   c. Undefined
   d. Undefined

105. _____ is a kind of property which exists as magnitude or multitude. It is among the basic classes of things along with quality, substance, change, and relation.
   a. Amount0
   b. Thing
   c. Undefined
   d. Undefined

106. In topology and related areas of mathematics a _____ or Moore-Smith sequence is a generalization of a sequence, intended to unify the various notions of limit and generalize them to arbitrary topological spaces.
   a. Thing
   b. Net0
   c. Undefined
   d. Undefined

107. In business, _____, _____ cost or _____ expense refers to an ongoing expense of operating a business.
   a. Thing
   b. Overhead0
   c. Undefined
   d. Undefined

108. In Euclidean geometry, a uniform _____ is a linear transformation that enlargers or diminishes objects, and whose _____ factor is the same in all directions. This is also called homothethy.
   a. Thing
   b. Scale0
   c. Undefined
   d. Undefined

109. _____ means "constancy", i.e. if something retains a certain feature even after we change a way of looking at it, then it is symmetric.
   a. Thing
   b. Symmetry0
   c. Undefined
   d. Undefined

110. In geometry, a _____ is a special kind of point, usually a corner of a polygon, polyhedron, or higher dimensional polytope. In the geometry of curves a _____ is a point of where the first derivative of curvature is zero. In graph theory, a _____ is the fundamental unit out of which graphs are formed
   a. Thing
   b. Vertex0
   c. Undefined
   d. Undefined

111. _____ is a technique used in algebra to solve quadratic equations, in analytic geometry for determining the shapes of graphs, and in calculus for computing integrals, including, but hardly limited to, the integrals that define Laplace transforms. The essential objective is to reduce a quadratic polynomial in a variable in an equation or expression to a squared polynomial of linear order. This can reduce an equation or integral to one that is more easily solved or evaluated.
   a. Thing
   b. Completing the square0
   c. Undefined
   d. Undefined

112. The _____ are the only integral domain whose positive elements are well-ordered, and in which order is preserved by addition. Like the natural numbers, the _____ form a countably infinite set. The set of all _____ is usually denoted in mathematics by a boldface Z .
   a. Integers0
   b. Thing
   c. Undefined
   d. Undefined

113. In mathematics, the _____ of two sets A and B is the set that contains all elements of A that also belong to B (or equivalently, all elements of B that also belong to A), but no other elements.
   a. Thing
   b. Intersection0
   c. Undefined
   d. Undefined

114. In geometry, the _____ of an object is a point in some sense in the middle of the object.
   a. Thing
   b. Center0
   c. Undefined
   d. Undefined

115. _____ is the flow of blood in the cardiovascular system.
   a. Thing
   b. Blood flow0
   c. Undefined
   d. Undefined

116. A _____ is a special kind of ratio, indicating a relationship between two measurements with different units, such as miles to gallons or cents to pounds.
   a. Thing
   b. Rate0
   c. Undefined
   d. Undefined

117. In mathematics, a _____ is the end result of a division problem. It can also be expressed as the number of times the divisor divides into the dividend.
   a. Quotlent0
   b. Thing
   c. Undefined
   d. Undefined

118. Acid _____ ratio measures the ability of a company to use its near cash or quick assets to immediately extinguish its current liabilities.
   a. Thing
   b. Test0
   c. Undefined
   d. Undefined

119. The function difference divided by the point difference is known as the _____
   a. Difference quotient0
   b. Thing
   c. Undefined
   d. Undefined

120. A _____ of a number is a number a such that $a^3 = x$.

Chapter 1. A Beginning Library of Elementary Functions

    a. Thing
    c. Undefined
    b. Cube root0
    d. Undefined

121. _____ is a term used in marketing to indicate how much the price of a product is above the cost of producing and distributing the product.
    a. Thing
    c. Undefined
    b. Markup0
    d. Undefined

122. A _____ is a plan of action to guide decisions and actions.
    a. Thing
    c. Undefined
    b. Policy0
    d. Undefined

123. Compass and straightedge or ruler-and-compass _____ is the _____ of lengths or angles using only an idealized ruler and compass.
    a. Thing
    c. Undefined
    b. Construction0
    d. Undefined

124. _____ is a regression method that models the relationship between a dependent variable Y, independent variables Xp, and a random term å.
    a. Linear regression0
    c. Undefined
    b. Thing
    d. Undefined

125. _____ the expected value of a random variable displays the average or central value of the variable. It is a summary value of the distribution of the variable.
    a. Thing
    c. Undefined
    b. Determining0
    d. Undefined

126. In mathematics, a _____ is a constant multiplicative factor of a certain object. The object can be such things as a variable, a vector, a function, etc. For example, the _____ of $9x^2$ is 9.
    a. Thing
    c. Undefined
    b. Coefficient0
    d. Undefined

127. A _____ is a landform that extends above the surrounding terrain in a limited area. A _____ is generally steeper than a hill, but there is no universally accepted standard definition for the height of a _____ or a hill although a _____ usually has an identifiable summit.
    a. Mountain0
    c. Undefined
    b. Thing
    d. Undefined

Chapter 2. Additional Elementary Functions

1. A _____ is a polynomial function of the form $f(x) = ax^2 + bx + c$, where a, b, c are real numbers and a , 0.
   a. Quadratic function0
   b. Event
   c. Undefined
   d. Undefined

2. The word _____ comes from the Latin word linearis, which means created by lines.
   a. Thing
   b. Linear0
   c. Undefined
   d. Undefined

3. In mathematics, a _____ is an expression that is constructed from one or more variables and constants, using only the operations of addition, subtraction, multiplication, and constant positive whole number exponents. is a _____. Note in particular that division by an expression containing a variable is not in general allowed in polynomials. [1]
   a. Polynomial0
   b. Thing
   c. Undefined
   d. Undefined

4. The mathematical concept of a _____ expresses the intuitive idea of deterministic dependence between two quantities, one of which is viewed as primary and the other as secondary. A _____ then is a way to associate a unique output for each input of a specified type, for example, a real number or an element of a given set.
   a. Thing
   b. Function0
   c. Undefined
   d. Undefined

5. The _____ integers are all the integers from zero on upwards.
   a. Thing
   b. Nonnegative0
   c. Undefined
   d. Undefined

6. In mathematics, a _____ may be described informally as a number that can be given by an infinite decimal representation.
   a. Real number0
   b. Thing
   c. Undefined
   d. Undefined

7. _____ is a function of the form
   a. Cubic function0
   b. Thing
   c. Undefined
   d. Undefined

8. In mathematics and the mathematical sciences, a _____ is a fixed, but possibly unspecified, value. This is in contrast to a variable, which is not fixed.
   a. Constant0
   b. Thing
   c. Undefined
   d. Undefined

9. _____ is a function whose values do not vary and thus are constant.
   a. Thing
   b. Constant function0
   c. Undefined
   d. Undefined

10. In mathematics, there are several meanings of _____ depending on the subject.
    a. Degree0
    b. Thing
    c. Undefined
    d. Undefined

Chapter 2. Additional Elementary Functions

11. In mathematics, a _____ is a constant multiplicative factor of a certain object. The object can be such things as a variable, a vector, a function, etc. For example, the _____ of $9x^2$ is 9.
    a. Coefficient0
    b. Thing
    c. Undefined
    d. Undefined

12. In mathematics, a _____ of a k-place relation $L \subseteq X_1 \times ... \times X_k$ is one of the sets X_j, $1 \leq j \leq k$. In the special case where k = 2 and $L \subseteq X_1 \times X_2$ is a function $L : X_1 \rightarrow X_2$, it is conventional to refer to X_1 as the _____ of the function and to refer to X_2 as the codomain of the function.
    a. Domain0
    b. Thing
    c. Undefined
    d. Undefined

13. _____ are external two-dimensional outlines, with the appearance or configuration of some thing - in contrast to the matter or content or substance of which it is composed.
    a. Thing
    b. Shapes0
    c. Undefined
    d. Undefined

14. _____ are the basic objects of study in graph theory. Informally speaking, a graph is a set of objects called points, nodes, or vertices connected by links called lines or edges.
    a. Graphs0
    b. Thing
    c. Undefined
    d. Undefined

15. An _____ is a straight line around which a geometric figure can be rotated.
    a. Axis0
    b. Thing
    c. Undefined
    d. Undefined

16. A _____ function is a function for which, intuitively, small changes in the input result in small changes in the output.
    a. Event
    b. Continuous0
    c. Undefined
    d. Undefined

17. In mathematics, a _____ is a statement that can be proved on the basis of explicitly stated or previously agreed assumptions.
    a. Theorem0
    b. Thing
    c. Undefined
    d. Undefined

18. _____ has many meanings, most of which simply .
    a. Power0
    b. Thing
    c. Undefined
    d. Undefined

19. Any point where a graph makes contact with an coordinate axis is called an _____ of the graph
    a. Intercept0
    b. Thing
    c. Undefined
    d. Undefined

20. _____ is a synonym for information.

Chapter 2. Additional Elementary Functions

a. Thing
b. Data0
c. Undefined
d. Undefined

21. A _____ is a first degree polynomial mathematical function of the form: f(x) = mx + b where m and b are real constants and x is a real variable.
a. Linear function0
b. Thing
c. Undefined
d. Undefined

22. In mathematics, the concept of a _____ tries to capture the intuitive idea of a geometrical one-dimensional and continuous object. A simple example is the circle.
a. Curve0
b. Thing
c. Undefined
d. Undefined

23. In mathematics, _____ are the intuitive idea of a geometrical one-dimensional and continuous object.
a. Thing
b. Curves0
c. Undefined
d. Undefined

24. The act of _____ is the calculated approximation of a result which is usable even if input data may be incomplete, uncertain, or noisy.
a. Thing
b. Estimating0
c. Undefined
d. Undefined

25. _____ is the fee paid on borrowed money.
a. Interest0
b. Thing
c. Undefined
d. Undefined

26. _____ is a regression method that models the relationship between a dependent variable Y, independent variables Xp, and a random term å.
a. Thing
b. Linear regression0
c. Undefined
d. Undefined

27. In mathematics, a _____ number is a number which can be expressed as a ratio of two integers. Non-integer _____ numbers (commonly called fractions) are usually written as the vulgar fraction a / b, where b is not zero.
a. Thing
b. Rational0
c. Undefined
d. Undefined

28. In mathematics, a _____ is any function which can be written as the ratio of two polynomial functions.
a. Rational function0
b. Thing
c. Undefined
d. Undefined

29. A _____ is the part of a fraction that tells how many equal parts make up a whole, and which is used in the name of the fraction: "halves", "thirds", "fourths" or "quarters", "fifths" and so on.
a. Concept
b. Denominator0
c. Undefined
d. Undefined

30. The _____ of a ring R is defined to be the smallest positive integer n such that $n a = 0$, for all a in R.

Chapter 2. Additional Elementary Functions

    a. Thing
    b. Characteristic0
    c. Undefined
    d. Undefined

31. In geographic information systems, a _____ comprises an entity with a geographic location, typically determined by points, arcs, or polygons. Carriageways and cadastres exemplify _____ data.
    a. Feature0
    b. Thing
    c. Undefined
    d. Undefined

32. Continuous functions are of utmost importance in mathematics and applications. However, not all functions are continuous. If a function is not continuous at a point in its domain, one says that it has a _____ there. The set of all points of _____ of a function may be a discrete set, a dense set, or even the entire domain of the function.
    a. Thing
    b. Discontinuity0
    c. Undefined
    d. Undefined

33. _____ is a straight line or curve A to which another curve B the one being studied approaches closer and closer as one moves along it.
    a. Vertical asymptote0
    b. Thing
    c. Undefined
    d. Undefined

34. An _____ is a straight line or curve A to which another curve B approaches closer and closer as one moves along it. As one moves along B, the space between it and the _____ A becomes smaller and smaller, and can in fact be made as small as one could wish by going far enough along. A curve may or may not touch or cross its _____. In fact, the curve may intersect the _____ an infinite number of times.
    a. Thing
    b. Asymptote0
    c. Undefined
    d. Undefined

35. A _____ is a numeral used to indicate a count. The most common use of the word today is to name the part of a fraction that tells the number or count of equal parts.
    a. Numerator0
    b. Thing
    c. Undefined
    d. Undefined

36. In astronomy, geography, geometry and related sciences and contexts, a plane is said to be _____ at a given point if it is locally perpendicular to the gradient of the gravity field, i.e., with the direction of the gravitational force at that point.
    a. Thing
    b. Horizontal0
    c. Undefined
    d. Undefined

37. In mathematics, the _____ of a coordinate system is the point where the axes of the system intersect.
    a. Thing
    b. Origin0
    c. Undefined
    d. Undefined

38. In mathematics, an _____, mean, or central tendency of a data set refers to a measure of the "middle" or "expected" value of the data set.
    a. Concept
    b. Average0
    c. Undefined
    d. Undefined

39. In mathematics, in the field of group theory, a _____ of a group is a quasisimple subnormal subgroup.

a. Component0
b. Concept
c. Undefined
d. Undefined

40. In finance, a _____ is collateral that the holder of a position in securities, options, or futures contracts has to deposit to cover the credit risk of his counterparty.
   a. Thing
   b. Margin0
   c. Undefined
   d. Undefined

41. In mathematics, the _____ is a conic section generated by the intersection of a right circular conical surface and a plane parallel to a generating straight line of that surface. It can also be defined as locus of points in a plane which are equidistant from a given point.
   a. Thing
   b. Parabola0
   c. Undefined
   d. Undefined

42. _____ is the application of tools and a processing medium to the transformation of raw materials into finished goods for sale.
   a. Thing
   b. Manufacturing0
   c. Undefined
   d. Undefined

43. Fixed costs are expenses whose total does not change in proportion to the activity of a business.Unit fixed costs decline with volume following a retangular hyperbola as the volume of production.Variable costs by contrast change in relation to the activity of a business such as sales or production volume.Along with variable costs,fixed costs make up one of the two components of total cost. In the most simple production function total cost is equal to fixed costs plus variable costs.In accounting terminology, fixed costs will broadly include all costs which are not included in cost of goods sold, and variable costs are those captured in costs of goods sold. The implicit assumption required to make the equivalence between the accounting and economics terminology is that the accounting period is equal to the period in which fixed costs do not vary in relation to production. In practice, this equivalence does not always hold and depending on the period under consideration by management, some overhead expenses can be adjusted by management, and the specific allocation of each expense to each category will be decided under cost accounting.In business planning and management accounting, usage of the terms fixed costs, variable costs and others will often differ from usage in economics, and may depend on the intended use. For example, costs may be segregated into per unit costs fixed costs per period, and variable costs as a proportion of revenue. Capital expenditures will usually be allocated separately, and depending on the purpose, a portion may be regularly allocated to expenses as depreciation and amortization and seen as a _____ per period, or the entire amount may be considered upfront fixed costs.
   a. Thing
   b. Fixed cost0
   c. Undefined
   d. Undefined

44. _____ are expenses whose total does not change in proportion to the activity of a business, within the relevant time period or scale of production
   a. Thing
   b. Fixed costs0
   c. Undefined
   d. Undefined

45. Initial objects are also called _____, and terminal objects are also called final.
   a. Thing
   b. Coterminal0
   c. Undefined
   d. Undefined

Chapter 2. Additional Elementary Functions

46. In linear algebra, the _____ of an n-by-n square matrix A is defined to be the sum of the elements on the main diagonal of A,
    a. Trace0
    b. Thing
    c. Undefined
    d. Undefined

47. In mathematics, a _____ is the result of multiplying, or an expression that identifies factors to be multiplied.
    a. Product0
    b. Thing
    c. Undefined
    d. Undefined

48. In economics, economic _____ is simply a state of the world where economic forces are balanced and in the absence of external influences the values of economic variables will not change.
    a. Equilibrium0
    b. Thing
    c. Undefined
    d. Undefined

49. _____ is the price at which the quantity demanded of a good or service is equal to the quantity supplied.
    a. Equilibrium price0
    b. Thing
    c. Undefined
    d. Undefined

50. In mathematics, the _____ of two sets A and B is the set that contains all elements of A that also belong to B (or equivalently, all elements of B that also belong to A), but no other elements.
    a. Intersection0
    b. Thing
    c. Undefined
    d. Undefined

51. In economics, supply and _____ describe market relations between prospective sellers and buyers of a good.
    a. Thing
    b. Demand0
    c. Undefined
    d. Undefined

52. In mathematics, _____ growth occurs when the growth rate of a function is always proportional to the function's current size.
    a. Exponential0
    b. Thing
    c. Undefined
    d. Undefined

53. A _____ is a symbolic representation denoting a quantity or expression. It often represents an "unknown" quantity that has the potential to change.
    a. Thing
    b. Variable0
    c. Undefined
    d. Undefined

54. _____ is one of the most important functions in mathematics. A function commonly used to study growth and decay
    a. Exponential function0
    b. Thing
    c. Undefined
    d. Undefined

55. In mathematics, the _____ of a function is the set of all "output" values produced by that function. Given a function $f : A \to B$, the _____ of f, is defined to be the set $\{x \in B : x = f(a) \text{ for some } a \in A\}$.

Chapter 2. Additional Elementary Functions

a. Range0
b. Thing
c. Undefined
d. Undefined

56. The _____ are the only integral domain whose positive elements are well-ordered, and in which order is preserved by addition. Like the natural numbers, the _____ form a countably infinite set. The set of all _____ is usually denoted in mathematics by a boldface Z .
   a. Integers0
   b. Thing
   c. Undefined
   d. Undefined

57. Equivalence is the condition of being _____ or essentially equal.
   a. Equivalent0
   b. Thing
   c. Undefined
   d. Undefined

58. _____ is a set of numbers, in the broadest sense of the word, together with one or more operations, such as addition or multiplication.
   a. Thing
   b. Number system0
   c. Undefined
   d. Undefined

59. A _____ is 360° or 2ð radians.
   a. Turn0
   b. Thing
   c. Undefined
   d. Undefined

60. _____ is a mathematical subject that includes the study of limits, derivatives, integrals, and power series and constitutes a major part of modern university curriculum.
   a. Thing
   b. Calculus0
   c. Undefined
   d. Undefined

61. In mathematics, a set is called _____ if there is a bijection between the set and some set of the form {1, 2, ..., n} where n is a natural number.
   a. Thing
   b. Finite0
   c. Undefined
   d. Undefined

62. In mathematics, an _____ number is any real number that is not a rational number- that is, it is a number which cannot be expressed as a fraction m/n, where m and n are integers.
   a. Thing
   b. Irrational0
   c. Undefined
   d. Undefined

63. In mathematics, an _____ is any real number that is not a rational number ¡ª that is, it is a number which cannot be expressed as m/n, where m and n are integers.
   a. Thing
   b. Irrational number0
   c. Undefined
   d. Undefined

64. An _____ is a combination of numbers, operators, grouping symbols and/or free variables and bound variables arranged in a meaningful way which can be evaluated..

Chapter 2. Additional Elementary Functions

    a. Thing
    b. Expression0
    c. Undefined
    d. Undefined

65. A _____ is a set of numbers that designate location in a given reference system, such as x,y in a planar _____ system or an x,y,z in a three-dimensional _____ system.
    a. Coordinate0
    b. Thing
    c. Undefined
    d. Undefined

66. Leonhard _____ was a pioneering Swiss mathematician and physicist, who spent most of his life in Russia and Germany.
    a. Euler0
    b. Person
    c. Undefined
    d. Undefined

67. An _____ is when two lines intersect somewhere on a plane creating a right angle at intersection
    a. Axes0
    b. Thing
    c. Undefined
    d. Undefined

68. _____ was a pioneering Swiss mathematician and physicist, who spent most of his life in Russia and Germany.
    a. Person
    b. Leonhard Euler0
    c. Undefined
    d. Undefined

69. In mathematics, _____ occurs when the growth rate of a function is always proportional to the function's current size.
    a. Thing
    b. Exponential growth0
    c. Undefined
    d. Undefined

70. _____ is a decrease that follows an exponential function.
    a. Thing
    b. Exponential decay0
    c. Undefined
    d. Undefined

71. A _____ is a special kind of ratio, indicating a relationship between two measurements with different units, such as miles to gallons or cents to pounds.
    a. Rate0
    b. Thing
    c. Undefined
    d. Undefined

72. _____ is a way of expressing a number as a fraction of 100 per cent meaning "per hundred".
    a. Thing
    b. Percent0
    c. Undefined
    d. Undefined

73. In business, particularly accounting, a _____ is the time intervals that the accounts, statement, payments, or other calculations cover.
    a. Thing
    b. Period0
    c. Undefined
    d. Undefined

74. An _____ is the fee paid on borrow money.

Chapter 2. Additional Elementary Functions

a. Concept
b. Interest rate0
c. Undefined
d. Undefined

75. _____ is a kind of property which exists as magnitude or multitude. It is among the basic classes of things along with quality, substance, change, and relation.
   a. Amount0
   b. Thing
   c. Undefined
   d. Undefined

76. _____ interest refers to the fact that whenever interest is calculated, it is based not only on the original principal, but also on any unpaid interest that has been added to the principal.
   a. Compound0
   b. Thing
   c. Undefined
   d. Undefined

77. _____ refers to the fact that whenever interest is calculated, it is based not only on the original principal, but also on any unpaid interest that has been added to the principal. The more frequently interest is compounded, the faster the balance grows.
   a. Compound interest0
   b. Concept
   c. Undefined
   d. Undefined

78. In elementary algebra, an _____ is a set that contains every real number between two indicated numbers and may contain the two numbers themselves.
   a. Thing
   b. Interval0
   c. Undefined
   d. Undefined

79. _____ studies and addresses the ways in which individuals, businesses, and organizations raise, allocate, and use monetary resources over time, taking into account the risks entailed in their projects
   a. Thing
   b. Finance0
   c. Undefined
   d. Undefined

80. _____ usually refers to money in the form of liquid currency, such as banknotes or coins.
   a. Thing
   b. Cash0
   c. Undefined
   d. Undefined

81. The _____ refers to a relationship between the duration of learning or experience and the resulting progress
   a. Learning curve0
   b. Thing
   c. Undefined
   d. Undefined

82. _____ are activities that are governed by a set of rules or customs and often engaged in competitively.
   a. Sports0
   b. Thing
   c. Undefined
   d. Undefined

83. A _____ is a form of periodic payment from an employer to an employee, which is specified in an employment contract.
   a. Salary0
   b. Thing
   c. Undefined
   d. Undefined

Chapter 2. Additional Elementary Functions

84. _____ is electromagnetic radiation with a wavelength that is visible to the eye (visible _____) or, in a technical or scientific context, electromagnetic radiation of any wavelength.
   a. Thing
   b. Light0
   c. Undefined
   d. Undefined

85. _____ is the level of functional and/or metabolic efficiency of an organism at both the micro level.
   a. Health0
   b. Thing
   c. Undefined
   d. Undefined

86. In epidemiology, an _____ is a disease that appears as new cases in a given human population, during a given period, at a rate that substantially exceeds with is "expected," based on recent experience.
   a. Epidemic0
   b. Thing
   c. Undefined
   d. Undefined

87. In sociology and biology a _____ is the collection of people or organisms of a particular species living in a given geographic area or space, usually measured by a census.
   a. Thing
   b. Population0
   c. Undefined
   d. Undefined

88. The _____ is the total number of human beings alive on the planet Earth at a given time.
   a. Thing
   b. World population0
   c. Undefined
   d. Undefined

89. _____ is change in population over time, and can be quantified as the change in the number of individuals in a population per unit time.
   a. Thing
   b. Population growth0
   c. Undefined
   d. Undefined

90. _____ element of an element x with respect to a binary operation * with identity element e is an element y such that x * y = y * x = e. In particular,
   a. Thing
   b. Inverse0
   c. Undefined
   d. Undefined

91. An _____ is a function which does the reverse of a given function.
   a. Inverse function0
   b. Thing
   c. Undefined
   d. Undefined

92. A _____ is a function for which, intuitively, small changes in the input result in small changes in the output.
   a. Continuous function0
   b. Event
   c. Undefined
   d. Undefined

93. In a function the _____, is the variable which is the value, i.e. the "output", of the function.
   a. Dependent variable0
   b. Thing
   c. Undefined
   d. Undefined

Chapter 2. Additional Elementary Functions

94. An _____ is a collection of two not necessarily distinct objects, one of which is distinguished as the first coordinate and the other as the second coordinate.
    a. Ordered pair0
    b. Thing
    c. Undefined
    d. Undefined

95. _____ means "constancy", i.e. if something retains a certain feature even after we change a way of looking at it, then it is symmetric.
    a. Symmetry0
    b. Thing
    c. Undefined
    d. Undefined

96. In mathematics, a _____ of a number x is the exponent y of the power by such that $x = b^y$. The value used for the base b must be neither 0 nor 1, nor a root of 1 in the case of the extension to complex numbers, and is typically 10, e, or 2.
    a. Thing
    b. Logarithm0
    c. Undefined
    d. Undefined

97. In mathematics, a _____ is a demonstration that, assuming certain axioms, some statement is necessarily true.
    a. Proof0
    b. Thing
    c. Undefined
    d. Undefined

98. _____ is the logarithm to the base e, where e is an irrational constant approximately equal to 2.718281828459.
    a. Natural logarithm0
    b. Thing
    c. Undefined
    d. Undefined

99. In mathematics, the _____ is the logarithm with base 10.
    a. Common logarithm0
    b. Thing
    c. Undefined
    d. Undefined

100. In mathematics, a _____ is a number in the form of a + bi where a and b are real numbers, and i is the imaginary unit, with the property $i^2 = -1$. The real number a is called the real part of the _____, and the real number b is the imaginary part.
    a. Complex number0
    b. Thing
    c. Undefined
    d. Undefined

101. _____ or investing is a term with several closely-related meanings in business management, finance and economics, related to saving or deferring consumption.
    a. Thing
    b. Investment0
    c. Undefined
    d. Undefined

102. The _____ is the period of time required for a quantity to double in size or value.
    a. Doubling time0
    b. Thing
    c. Undefined
    d. Undefined

103. A _____ is a negotiable instrument instructing a financial institution to pay a specific amount of a specific currency from a specific demand account held in the maker/depositor's name with that institution. Both the maker and payee may be natural persons or legal entities.

Chapter 2. Additional Elementary Functions

- a. Check0
- b. Thing
- c. Undefined
- d. Undefined

104. The _____, the average in everyday English, which is also called the arithmetic _____ (and is distinguished from the geometric _____ or harmonic _____). The average is also called the sample _____. The expected value of a random variable, which is also called the population _____.
- a. Mean0
- b. Thing
- c. Undefined
- d. Undefined

105. In finance and economics, _____ is the process of finding the present value of an amount of cash at some future date, and along with compounding cash forms the basis of time value of money calculations.
- a. Thing
- b. Discount0
- c. Undefined
- d. Undefined

106. The _____, i.e., acoustic intensity is defined as the sound power P_{ac} per unit area A.
- a. Sound intensity0
- b. Thing
- c. Undefined
- d. Undefined

107. The _____ relative to a specified or implied reference level.
- a. Decibel0
- b. Thing
- c. Undefined
- d. Undefined

108. A _____ is a function that assigns a number to subsets of a given set.
- a. Thing
- b. Measure0
- c. Undefined
- d. Undefined

109. In Euclidean geometry, a uniform _____ is a linear transformation that enlargers or diminishes objects, and whose _____ factor is the same in all directions. This is also called homothethy.
- a. Thing
- b. Scale0
- c. Undefined
- d. Undefined

110. In mathematics, a _____ of a complex-valued function f is a member x of the domain of f such that f(x) vanishes at x, that is, $x : f(x) = 0$.
- a. Root0
- b. Thing
- c. Undefined
- d. Undefined

111. _____ of a single or multiple future payments is the nominal amounts of money to change hands at some future date, discounted to account for the time value of money, and other factors such as investment risk.
- a. Present value0
- b. Thing
- c. Undefined
- d. Undefined

112. _____ measures the nominal future sum of money that a given sum of money is "worth" at a specified time in the future assuming a certain interest rate; this value does not include corrections for inflation or other factors that affect the true value of money in the future.

a. Thing
b. Future value0
c. Undefined
d. Undefined

113. In mathematics, the conjugate _____ or adjoint matrix of an m-by-n matrix A with complex entries is the n-by-m matrix A* obtained from A by taking the transpose and then taking the complex conjugate of each entry.
a. Thing
b. Pairs0
c. Undefined
d. Undefined

114. _____ is the estimation of a physical quantity such as distance, energy, temperature, or time.
a. Thing
b. Measurement0
c. Undefined
d. Undefined

115. In mathematics and its applications, a _____ is a system for assigning an n-tuple of numbers or scalars to each point in an n-dimensional space.
a. Coordinate system0
b. Concept
c. Undefined
d. Undefined

116. In plane geometry, a _____ is a polygon with four equal sides, four right angles, and parallel opposite sides. In algebra, the _____ of a number is that number multiplied by itself.
a. Square0
b. Thing
c. Undefined
d. Undefined

117. In mathematics, a _____ set is the complement of a meager set. A meager set is one which is the countable union of nowhere dense sets.
a. Thing
b. Residual0
c. Undefined
d. Undefined

118. A _____ is the result of the addition of a set of numbers. The numbers may be natural numbers, complex numbers, matrices, or still more complicated objects. An infinite _____ is a subtle procedure known as a series.
a. Sum0
b. Thing
c. Undefined
d. Undefined

119. In common philosophical language, a proposition or _____, is the content of an assertion, that is, it is true-or-false and defined by the meaning of a particular piece of language.
a. Statement0
b. Concept
c. Undefined
d. Undefined

Chapter 3. The Derivative

1. A _____ is a symbolic representation denoting a quantity or expression. It often represents an "unknown" quantity that has the potential to change.
   - a. Thing
   - b. Variable0
   - c. Undefined
   - d. Undefined

2. _____ is a branch of mathematics concerning the study of structure, relation and quantity.
   - a. Concept
   - b. Algebra0
   - c. Undefined
   - d. Undefined

3. _____ is a mathematical subject that includes the study of limits, derivatives, integrals, and power series and constitutes a major part of modern university curriculum.
   - a. Thing
   - b. Calculus0
   - c. Undefined
   - d. Undefined

4. Sir Isaac _____, was an English physicist, mathematician, astronomer, natural philosopher, and alchemist, regarded by many as the greatest figure in the history of science
   - a. Newton0
   - b. Person
   - c. Undefined
   - d. Undefined

5. _____ was a German polymath who wrote mostly in Latin and French.
   - a. Thing
   - b. Gottfried Wilhelm von Leibniz0
   - c. Undefined
   - d. Undefined

6. _____ was a German mathematician and philosopher. He invented calculus independently of Newton, and his notation is the one in general use since.
   - a. Leibniz0
   - b. Person
   - c. Undefined
   - d. Undefined

7. Sir _____ was an English physicist, mathematician, astronomer, natural philosopher, and alchemist, regarded by many as the greatest figure in the history of science.
   - a. Isaac Newton0
   - b. Person
   - c. Undefined
   - d. Undefined

8. In mathematics, an _____, mean, or central tendency of a data set refers to a measure of the "middle" or "expected" value of the data set.
   - a. Average0
   - b. Concept
   - c. Undefined
   - d. Undefined

9. _____ is a business term for the amount of money that a company receives from its activities in a given period, mostly from sales of products and/or services to customers
   - a. Revenue0
   - b. Thing
   - c. Undefined
   - d. Undefined

10. A _____ is a special kind of ratio, indicating a relationship between two measurements with different units, such as miles to gallons or cents to pounds.

a. Rate0
b. Thing
c. Undefined
d. Undefined

11. A _____ is a quantity that denotes the proportional amount or magnitude of one quantity relative to another.
   a. Ratio0
   b. Thing
   c. Undefined
   d. Undefined

12. The mathematical concept of a _____ expresses the intuitive idea of deterministic dependence between two quantities, one of which is viewed as primary and the other as secondary. A _____ then is a way to associate a unique output for each input of a specified type, for example, a real number or an element of a given set.
   a. Thing
   b. Function0
   c. Undefined
   d. Undefined

13. In mathematics, a _____ is the end result of a division problem. It can also be expressed as the number of times the divisor divides into the dividend.
   a. Quotient0
   b. Thing
   c. Undefined
   d. Undefined

14. An _____ is a combination of numbers, operators, grouping symbols and/or free variables and bound variables arranged in a meaningful way which can be evaluated..
   a. Thing
   b. Expression0
   c. Undefined
   d. Undefined

15. The function difference divided by the point difference is known as the _____
   a. Thing
   b. Difference quotient0
   c. Undefined
   d. Undefined

16. _____ of an object is its speed in a particular direction.
   a. Thing
   b. Velocity0
   c. Undefined
   d. Undefined

17. A _____ is a set of numbers that designate location in a given reference system, such as x,y in a planar _____ system or an x,y,z in a three-dimensional _____ system.
   a. Coordinate0
   b. Thing
   c. Undefined
   d. Undefined

18. _____, Greek for "knowledge of nature," is the branch of science concerned with the discovery and characterization of universal laws which govern matter, energy, space, and time.
   a. Physics0
   b. Thing
   c. Undefined
   d. Undefined

19. In elementary algebra, an _____ is a set that contains every real number between two indicated numbers and may contain the two numbers themselves.
   a. Thing
   b. Interval0
   c. Undefined
   d. Undefined

Chapter 3. The Derivative

20. A _____ is a deliberate process for transforming one or more inputs into one or more results.
    a. Thing
    b. Calculation0
    c. Undefined
    d. Undefined

21. In mathematics, an _____ is any of the arguments, i.e. "inputs", to a function. Thus if we have a function f(x), then x is a _____.
    a. Thing
    b. Independent variable0
    c. Undefined
    d. Undefined

22. In a function the _____, is the variable which is the value, i.e. the "output", of the function.
    a. Dependent variable0
    b. Thing
    c. Undefined
    d. Undefined

23. _____ is often used to describe the measurement of the steepness, incline, gradient, or grade of a straight line. The _____ is defined as the ratio of the "rise" divided by the "run" between two points on a line, or in other words, the ratio of the altitude change to the horizontal distance between any two points on the line.
    a. Slope0
    b. Thing
    c. Undefined
    d. Undefined

24. In mathematics, the _____ f is the collection of all ordered pairs . In particular, graph means the graphical representation of this collection, in the form of a curve or surface, together with axes, etc. Graphing on a Cartesian plane is sometimes referred to as curve sketching.
    a. Graph of a function0
    b. Thing
    c. Undefined
    d. Undefined

25. _____ of a curve is a line that intersects two or more points on the curve.
    a. Thing
    b. Secant line0
    c. Undefined
    d. Undefined

26. _____ is a trigonometric function that is the reciprocal of cosine.
    a. Secant0
    b. Thing
    c. Undefined
    d. Undefined

27. _____ are the basic objects of study in graph theory. Informally speaking, a graph is a set of objects called points, nodes, or vertices connected by links called lines or edges.
    a. Graphs0
    b. Thing
    c. Undefined
    d. Undefined

28. In trigonometry, the _____ is a function defined as $\tan x = {\sin x}/{\cos x}$. The function is so-named because it can be defined as the length of a certain segment of a _____ (in the geometric sense) to the unit circle. In plane geometry, a line is _____ to a curve, at some point, if both line and curve pass through the point with the same direction.
    a. Tangent0
    b. Thing
    c. Undefined
    d. Undefined

29. In Euclidean geometry, a _____ is the set of all points in a plane at a fixed distance, called the radius, from a given point, the center.

a. Thing	b. Circle0
c. Undefined	d. Undefined

30. _____ has two distinct but etymologically-related meanings: one in geometry and one in trigonometry.
a. Thing	b. Tangent line0
c. Undefined	d. Undefined

31. In mathematics, a _____ is a two-dimensional manifold or surface that is perfectly flat.
a. Plane0	b. Thing
c. Undefined	d. Undefined

32. An _____ is a straight line around which a geometric figure can be rotated.
a. Thing	b. Axis0
c. Undefined	d. Undefined

33. In linear algebra, the _____ of an n-by-n square matrix A is defined to be the sum of the elements on the main diagonal of A,
a. Thing	b. Trace0
c. Undefined	d. Undefined

34. The word _____ comes from the Latin word linearis, which means created by lines.
a. Linear0	b. Thing
c. Undefined	d. Undefined

35. A _____ is a first degree polynomial mathematical function of the form: f(x) = mx + b where m and b are real constants and x is a real variable.
a. Linear function0	b. Thing
c. Undefined	d. Undefined

36. In astronomy, geography, geometry and related sciences and contexts, a plane is said to be _____ at a given point if it is locally perpendicular to the gradient of the gravity field, i.e., with the direction of the gravitational force at that point.
a. Horizontal0	b. Thing
c. Undefined	d. Undefined

37. In mathematics and the mathematical sciences, a _____ is a fixed, but possibly unspecified, value. This is in contrast to a variable, which is not fixed.
a. Constant0	b. Thing
c. Undefined	d. Undefined

38. _____ is a function whose values do not vary and thus are constant.
a. Thing	b. Constant function0
c. Undefined	d. Undefined

39. _____, from Latin meaning "to make progress", is defined in two different ways. Pure economic _____ is the increase in wealth that an investor has from making an investment, taking into consideration all costs associated with that investment including the opportunity cost of capital.

a. Thing
b. Profit0
c. Undefined
d. Undefined

40. In mathematics a _____ is a function which defines a distance between elements of a set.
    a. Metric0
    b. Thing
    c. Undefined
    d. Undefined

41. Compass and straightedge or ruler-and-compass _____ is the _____ of lengths or angles using only an idealized ruler and compass.
    a. Construction0
    b. Thing
    c. Undefined
    d. Undefined

42. A _____ is a numeral used to indicate a count. The most common use of the word today is to name the part of a fraction that tells the number or count of equal parts.
    a. Thing
    b. Numerator0
    c. Undefined
    d. Undefined

43. A _____ is the part of a fraction that tells how many equal parts make up a whole, and which is used in the name of the fraction: "halves", "thirds", "fourths" or "quarters", "fifths" and so on.
    a. Denominator0
    b. Concept
    c. Undefined
    d. Undefined

44. In physics, _____ is an influence that may cause an object to accelerate. It may be experienced as a lift, a push, or a pull. The actual acceleration of the body is determined by the vector sum of all forces acting on it, known as net _____ or resultant _____.
    a. Force0
    b. Thing
    c. Undefined
    d. Undefined

45. The _____, the average in everyday English, which is also called the arithmetic _____ (and is distinguished from the geometric _____ or harmonic _____). The average is also called the sample _____. The expected value of a random variable, which is also called the population _____.
    a. Mean0
    b. Thing
    c. Undefined
    d. Undefined

46. A _____ is the quantity that defines certain relatively constant characteristics of systems or functions..
    a. Parameter0
    b. Thing
    c. Undefined
    d. Undefined

47. _____ is the state of being greater than any finite real or natural number, however large.
    a. Infinite0
    b. Thing
    c. Undefined
    d. Undefined

48. In set theory, an _____ is a set that is not a finite set. Infinite sets may be countable or uncountable.
    a. Thing
    b. Infinite set0
    c. Undefined
    d. Undefined

Chapter 3. The Derivative

49. In mathematics, a set is called _____ if there is a bijection between the set and some set of the form {1, 2, ..., n} where n is a natural number.
   a. Finite0
   b. Thing
   c. Undefined
   d. Undefined

50. In mathematics, a _____ occurs if there is a bijection between the set and some set of the form 1, 2, ..., n where n is a natural number.
   a. Concept
   b. Finite set0
   c. Undefined
   d. Undefined

51. _____ is the middle point of a line segment.
   a. Thing
   b. Midpoint0
   c. Undefined
   d. Undefined

52. In mathematics, a _____ may be described informally as a number that can be given by an infinite decimal representation.
   a. Thing
   b. Real number0
   c. Undefined
   d. Undefined

53. In mathematics, the term _____ is applied to certain functions. There are two common ways it is applied: these are related historically, but diverged somewhat during the twentieth century.
   a. Thing
   b. Functional0
   c. Undefined
   d. Undefined

54. In mathematics, a _____ is a statement that can be proved on the basis of explicitly stated or previously agreed assumptions.
   a. Theorem0
   b. Thing
   c. Undefined
   d. Undefined

55. In calculus and other branches of mathematical analysis, an _____ is an algebraic expression obtained in the context of limits.
   a. Thing
   b. Indeterminate form0
   c. Undefined
   d. Undefined

56. _____ is the transport of people on a trip/journey or the process or time involved in a person or object moving from one location to another.
   a. Travel0
   b. Thing
   c. Undefined
   d. Undefined

57. There are two simple _____ the greatest common factor and least common multiple: standard factorization and prime factorization.
   a. Thing
   b. Methods for finding0
   c. Undefined
   d. Undefined

58. An _____ of a product of sums expresses it as a sum of products by using the fact that multiplication distributes over addition.

Chapter 3. The Derivative

    a. Expansion0
    c. Undefined
    b. Thing
    d. Undefined

59. When _____ symmetry one can determine whether or not an object is symmetric with respect to a given mathematical operation, if, when applied to the object, this operation does not change the object or its appearance.
    a. Investigating0
    c. Undefined
    b. Thing
    d. Undefined

60. The _____ are the only integral domain whose positive elements are well-ordered, and in which order is preserved by addition. Like the natural numbers, the _____ form a countably infinite set. The set of all _____ is usually denoted in mathematics by a boldface Z .
    a. Thing
    c. Undefined
    b. Integers0
    d. Undefined

61. In set theory and other branches of mathematics, the _____ of a collection of sets is the set that contains everything that belongs to any of the sets, but nothing else.
    a. Union0
    c. Undefined
    b. Thing
    d. Undefined

62. In geometry, an _____ of a triangle is a straight line through a vertex and perpendicular to (i.e. forming a right angle with) the opposite side or an extension of the opposite side.
    a. Concept
    c. Undefined
    b. Altitude0
    d. Undefined

63. A _____ is a function that assigns a number to subsets of a given set.
    a. Measure0
    c. Undefined
    b. Thing
    d. Undefined

64. _____ is a kind of property which exists as magnitude or multitude. It is among the basic classes of things along with quality, substance, change, and relation.
    a. Thing
    c. Undefined
    b. Amount0
    d. Undefined

65. In sociology and biology a _____ is the collection of people or organisms of a particular species living in a given geographic area or space, usually measured by a census.
    a. Population0
    c. Undefined
    b. Thing
    d. Undefined

66. The _____ is a measurement of how a function changes when the values of its inputs change.
    a. Thing
    c. Undefined
    b. Derivative0
    d. Undefined

67. _____, a field in mathematics, is the study of how functions change when their inputs change. The primary object of study in _____ is the derivative.

Chapter 3. The Derivative

a. Thing
b. Differential calculus0
c. Undefined
d. Undefined

68. A _____ is a set whose members are members of another set or a set contained within another set.
a. Subset0
b. Thing
c. Undefined
d. Undefined

69. In mathematics, a _____ of a k-place relation $L \subseteq X_1 \times \ldots \times X_k$ is one of the sets X_j, $1 \leq j \leq k$. In the special case where k = 2 and $L \subseteq X_1 \times X_2$ is a function $L : X_1 \to X_2$, it is conventional to refer to X_1 as the _____ of the function and to refer to X_2 as the codomain of the function.
a. Domain0
b. Thing
c. Undefined
d. Undefined

70. An _____ is when two lines intersect somewhere on a plane creating a right angle at intersection
a. Axes0
b. Thing
c. Undefined
d. Undefined

71. _____ is a technique of numerical analysis to produce an estimate of the derivative of a mathematical function or function subroutine using values from the function and perhaps other knowledge about the function.
a. Thing
b. Numerical differentiation0
c. Undefined
d. Undefined

72. A _____ is a negotiable instrument instructing a financial institution to pay a specific amount of a specific currency from a specific demand account held in the maker/depositor's name with that institution. Both the maker and payee may be natural persons or legal entities.
a. Check0
b. Thing
c. Undefined
d. Undefined

73. A _____ function is a function for which, intuitively, small changes in the input result in small changes in the output.
a. Event
b. Continuous0
c. Undefined
d. Undefined

74. _____ Any process by which a specified characteristic usually amplitude of the output of a device is prevented from exceeding a predetermined value.
a. Thing
b. Limiting0
c. Undefined
d. Undefined

75. In mathematics, a _____ is a countable collection of open covers of a topological space that satisfies certain separation axioms.
a. Thing
b. Development0
c. Undefined
d. Undefined

76. In common philosophical language, a proposition or _____, is the content of an assertion, that is, it is true-or-false and defined by the meaning of a particular piece of language.

a. Statement0
b. Concept
c. Undefined
d. Undefined

77. _____ is the fee paid on borrowed money.
   a. Thing
   b. Interest0
   c. Undefined
   d. Undefined

78. In business, particularly accounting, a _____ is the time intervals that the accounts, statement, payments, or other calculations cover.
   a. Thing
   b. Period0
   c. Undefined
   d. Undefined

79. _____ is a synonym for information.
   a. Thing
   b. Data0
   c. Undefined
   d. Undefined

80. _____ is a temperature scale named after the German physicist Daniel Gabriel _____ , who proposed it in 1724.
   a. Thing
   b. Fahrenheit0
   c. Undefined
   d. Undefined

81. In mathematics, there are several meanings of _____ depending on the subject.
   a. Thing
   b. Degree0
   c. Undefined
   d. Undefined

82. _____ is a physical property of a system that underlies the common notions of hot and cold; something that is hotter has the greater _____.
   a. Thing
   b. Temperature0
   c. Undefined
   d. Undefined

83. _____ are objects, characters, or other concrete representations of ideas, concepts, or other abstractions.
   a. Thing
   b. Symbols0
   c. Undefined
   d. Undefined

84. _____ has many meanings, most of which simply .
   a. Thing
   b. Power0
   c. Undefined
   d. Undefined

85. In mathematics, a _____ is a constant multiplicative factor of a certain object. The object can be such things as a variable, a vector, a function, etc. For example, the _____ of $9x^2$ is 9.
   a. Thing
   b. Coefficient0
   c. Undefined
   d. Undefined

86. _____ is a method for differentiating expressions involving exponentiation the power operation.

Chapter 3. The Derivative

a. Thing
b. Power rule0
c. Undefined
d. Undefined

87. _____ is a mathematical operation, written a^n, involving two numbers, the base a and the exponent n.
  a. Exponentiating0
  b. Thing
  c. Undefined
  d. Undefined

88. _____ is a mathematical operation, written a^n, involving two numbers, the base a and the exponent n.
  a. Thing
  b. Exponentiation0
  c. Undefined
  d. Undefined

89. A _____ is the result of the addition of a set of numbers. The numbers may be natural numbers, complex numbers, matrices, or still more complicated objects. An infinite _____ is a subtle procedure known as a series.
  a. Thing
  b. Sum0
  c. Undefined
  d. Undefined

90. In mathematics, a _____ is an expression that is constructed from one or more variables and constants, using only the operations of addition, subtraction, multiplication, and constant positive whole number exponents. is a _____. Note in particular that division by an expression containing a variable is not in general allowed in polynomials. [1]
  a. Thing
  b. Polynomial0
  c. Undefined
  d. Undefined

91. _____ is the change in total cost that arises when the quantity produced changes by one unit.
  a. Marginal cost0
  b. Thing
  c. Undefined
  d. Undefined

92. In mathematics, the _____ is a conic section generated by the intersection of a right circular conical surface and a plane parallel to a generating straight line of that surface. It can also be defined as locus of points in a plane which are equidistant from a given point.
  a. Parabola0
  b. Thing
  c. Undefined
  d. Undefined

93. In geometry, a _____ is a special kind of point, usually a corner of a polygon, polyhedron, or higher dimensional polytope. In the geometry of curves a _____ is a point of where the first derivative of curvature is zero. In graph theory, a _____ is the fundamental unit out of which graphs are formed
  a. Vertex0
  b. Thing
  c. Undefined
  d. Undefined

94. In mathematics, a _____ is the result of multiplying, or an expression that identifies factors to be multiplied.
  a. Product0
  b. Thing
  c. Undefined
  d. Undefined

95. The plus and _____ signs are mathematical symbols used to represent the notions of positive and negative as well as the operations of addition and subtraction.

a. Thing
b. Minus0
c. Undefined
d. Undefined

96. The _____ is a method of finding the derivative of a function that is the quotient of two other functions for which derivatives exist.
   a. Quotient rule0
   b. Thing
   c. Undefined
   d. Undefined

97. In mathematics, _____ is an elementary arithmetic operation. When one of the numbers is a whole number, _____ is the repeated sum of the other number.
   a. Multiplication0
   b. Thing
   c. Undefined
   d. Undefined

98. The _____ governs the differentiation of products of differentiable functions.
   a. Product rule0
   b. Thing
   c. Undefined
   d. Undefined

99. In mathematics, _____ expressions is used to reduce the expression into the lowest possible term.
   a. Simplifying0
   b. Thing
   c. Undefined
   d. Undefined

100. In mathematics, a subset of Euclidean space R^n is called _____ if it is closed and bounded.
   a. Compact0
   b. Thing
   c. Undefined
   d. Undefined

101. _____ are procedures that allow people to exchange information by one of several methods.
   a. Thing
   b. Communications0
   c. Undefined
   d. Undefined

102. In economics, supply and _____ describe market relations between prospective sellers and buyers of a good.
   a. Thing
   b. Demand0
   c. Undefined
   d. Undefined

103. _____ was a U.S. pioneer in the fields of psychometrics and psychophysics. He conceived the approach to measurement known as the law of comparative judgment, and is well known for his contributions to factor analysis.
   a. Thurstone0
   b. Person
   c. Undefined
   d. Undefined

104. In calculus, the _____ is a formula for the derivative of the composite of two functions.
   a. Chain rule0
   b. Concept
   c. Undefined
   d. Undefined

105. In statistics, a _____ measure is one which is measuring what is supposed to measure.
   a. Thing
   b. Valid0
   c. Undefined
   d. Undefined

106. An _____ is the fee paid on borrow money.
a. Concept
b. Interest rate0
c. Undefined
d. Undefined

107. _____ is the level of functional and/or metabolic efficiency of an organism at both the micro level.
a. Thing
b. Health0
c. Undefined
d. Undefined

108. _____ is the use of marginal concepts within economics. Marginal concepts include marginal cost, marginal productivity and marginal utility, the law of diminishing rates of substitution, and the law of diminishing marginal utility.
a. Marginal analysis0
b. Thing
c. Undefined
d. Undefined

109. _____ is the extra revenue that an additional unit of product will bring a firm. It can also be described as the change in total revenue/change in number of units sold.
a. Marginal revenue0
b. Thing
c. Undefined
d. Undefined

110. In mathematics and its applications, a _____ is a system for assigning an n-tuple of numbers or scalars to each point in an n-dimensional space.
a. Coordinate system0
b. Concept
c. Undefined
d. Undefined

111. In mathematics, the _____ of two sets A and B is the set that contains all elements of A that also belong to B (or equivalently, all elements of B that also belong to A), but no other elements.
a. Thing
b. Intersection0
c. Undefined
d. Undefined

112. The _____ integers are all the integers from zero on upwards.
a. Nonnegative0
b. Thing
c. Undefined
d. Undefined

113. Any point where a graph makes contact with an coordinate axis is called an _____ of the graph
a. Intercept0
b. Thing
c. Undefined
d. Undefined

114. _____ is the application of tools and a processing medium to the transformation of raw materials into finished goods for sale.
a. Manufacturing0
b. Thing
c. Undefined
d. Undefined

115. The _____ of measurement are a globally standardized and modernized form of the metric system.
a. Units0
b. Thing
c. Undefined
d. Undefined

116. Fixed costs are expenses whose total does not change in proportion to the activity of a business.Unit fixed costs decline with volume following a retangular hyperbola as the volume of production.Variable costs by contrast change in relation to the activity of a business such as sales or production volume.Along with variable costs,fixed costs make up one of the two components of total cost. In the most simple production function total cost is equal to fixed costs plus variable costs.In accounting terminology, fixed costs will broadly include all costs which are not included in cost of goods sold, and variable costs are those captured in costs of goods sold. The implicit assumption required to make the equivalence between the accounting and economics terminology is that the accounting period is equal to the period in which fixed costs do not vary in relation to production. In practice, this equivalence does not always hold and depending on the period under consideration by management, some overhead expenses can be adjusted by management, and the specific allocation of each expense to each category will be decided under cost accounting.In business planning and management accounting, usage of the terms fixed costs, variable costs and others will often differ from usage in economics, and may depend on the intended use. For example, costs may be segregated into per unit costs fixed costs per period, and variable costs as a proportion of revenue. Capital expenditures will usually be allocated separately, and depending on the purpose, a portion may be regularly allocated to expenses as depreciation and amortization and seen as a _____ per period, or the entire amount may be considered upfront fixed costs.
- a. Fixed cost0
- b. Thing
- c. Undefined
- d. Undefined

117. _____ are expenses whose total does not change in proportion to the activity of a business, within the relevant time period or scale of production
- a. Thing
- b. Fixed costs0
- c. Undefined
- d. Undefined

118. _____ is a regression method that models the relationship between a dependent variable Y, independent variables Xp, and a random term å.
- a. Thing
- b. Linear regression0
- c. Undefined
- d. Undefined

119. In mathematics, the _____ of a function is the set of all "output" values produced by that function. Given a function $f : A \to B$, the _____ of f, is defined to be the set $\{x \in B : x = f(a) \text{ for some } a \in A\}$.
- a. Range0
- b. Thing
- c. Undefined
- d. Undefined

120. In mathematics, the _____ (or modulus) of a real number is its numerical value without regard to its sign.
- a. Absolute value0
- b. Thing
- c. Undefined
- d. Undefined

121. Mathematical _____ is used to represent ideas.
- a. Notation0
- b. Thing
- c. Undefined
- d. Undefined

122. In a mathematical proof or a syllogism, a _____ is a statement that is the logical consequence of preceding statements.
- a. Conclusion0
- b. Concept
- c. Undefined
- d. Undefined

123. In mathematics, in the field of group theory, a _____ of a group is a quasisimple subnormal subgroup.
   a. Concept
   b. Component0
   c. Undefined
   d. Undefined

124. In geometry, the _____ of an object is a point in some sense in the middle of the object.
   a. Thing
   b. Center0
   c. Undefined
   d. Undefined

125. A _____ is a unit of length, usually used to measure distance, in a number of different systems, including Imperial units, United States customary units and Norwegian/Swedish mil. Its size can vary from system to system, but in each is between 1 and 10 kilometers. In contemporary English contexts _____ refers to either:
   a. Mile0
   b. Thing
   c. Undefined
   d. Undefined

126. A _____ is a polynomial function of the form f(x) = ax^2 + bx +c , where a, b, c are real numbers and a , 0.
   a. Quadratic function0
   b. Event
   c. Undefined
   d. Undefined

127. _____ is a function of the form
   a. Thing
   b. Cubic function0
   c. Undefined
   d. Undefined

128. In geographic information systems, a _____ comprises an entity with a geographic location, typically determined by points, arcs, or polygons. Carriageways and cadastres exemplify _____ data.
   a. Feature0
   b. Thing
   c. Undefined
   d. Undefined

Chapter 4. Graphing and Optimization

1. In mathematics, the _____ f is the collection of all ordered pairs. In particular, graph means the graphical representation of this collection, in the form of a curve or surface, together with axes, etc. Graphing on a Cartesian plane is sometimes referred to as curve sketching.
   a. Graph of a function0
   b. Thing
   c. Undefined
   d. Undefined

2. The mathematical concept of a _____ expresses the intuitive idea of deterministic dependence between two quantities, one of which is viewed as primary and the other as secondary. A _____ then is a way to associate a unique output for each input of a specified type, for example, a real number or an element of a given set.
   a. Function0
   b. Thing
   c. Undefined
   d. Undefined

3. In computer science, an _____ is the problem of finding the best solution from all feasible solutions.
   a. Optimization problem0
   b. Thing
   c. Undefined
   d. Undefined

4. _____ is a mathematical subject that includes the study of limits, derivatives, integrals, and power series and constitutes a major part of modern university curriculum.
   a. Thing
   b. Calculus0
   c. Undefined
   d. Undefined

5. _____ are the basic objects of study in graph theory. Informally speaking, a graph is a set of objects called points, nodes, or vertices connected by links called lines or edges.
   a. Graphs0
   b. Thing
   c. Undefined
   d. Undefined

6. A _____ function is a function for which, intuitively, small changes in the input result in small changes in the output.
   a. Continuous0
   b. Event
   c. Undefined
   d. Undefined

7. In elementary algebra, an _____ is a set that contains every real number between two indicated numbers and may contain the two numbers themselves.
   a. Thing
   b. Interval0
   c. Undefined
   d. Undefined

8. Continuous functions are of utmost importance in mathematics and applications. However, not all functions are continuous. If a function is not continuous at a point in its domain, one says that it has a _____ there. The set of all points of _____ of a function may be a discrete set, a dense set, or even the entire domain of the function.
   a. Discontinuity0
   b. Thing
   c. Undefined
   d. Undefined

9. In business, particularly accounting, a _____ is the time intervals that the accounts, statement, payments, or other calculations cover.
   a. Thing
   b. Period0
   c. Undefined
   d. Undefined

Chapter 4. Graphing and Optimization

10. _____ is a physical property of a system that underlies the common notions of hot and cold; something that is hotter has the greater _____.
    a. Thing
    b. Temperature0
    c. Undefined
    d. Undefined

11. _____ is a list of goods and materials, or those goods and materials themselves, held available in stock by a business
    a. Inventory0
    b. Thing
    c. Undefined
    d. Undefined

12. In mathematics, _____ geometry was the traditional name for the geometry of three-dimensional Euclidean space — for practical purposes the kind of space we live in.
    a. Solid0
    b. Thing
    c. Undefined
    d. Undefined

13. In mathematics, a _____ is a statement that can be proved on the basis of explicitly stated or previously agreed assumptions.
    a. Theorem0
    b. Thing
    c. Undefined
    d. Undefined

14. In mathematics and the mathematical sciences, a _____ is a fixed, but possibly unspecified, value. This is in contrast to a variable, which is not fixed.
    a. Constant0
    b. Thing
    c. Undefined
    d. Undefined

15. _____ is a function whose values do not vary and thus are constant.
    a. Constant function0
    b. Thing
    c. Undefined
    d. Undefined

16. In mathematics, a _____ is an expression that is constructed from one or more variables and constants, using only the operations of addition, subtraction, multiplication, and constant positive whole number exponents. is a _____. Note in particular that division by an expression containing a variable is not in general allowed in polynomials. [1]
    a. Polynomial0
    b. Thing
    c. Undefined
    d. Undefined

17. In mathematics, an inequality is a statement about the relative size or order of two objects. For example 14 > 10, or 14 is _____ 10.
    a. Thing
    b. Greater than0
    c. Undefined
    d. Undefined

18. In mathematics, a _____ number is a number which can be expressed as a ratio of two integers. Non-integer _____ numbers (commonly called fractions) are usually written as the vulgar fraction a / b, where b is not zero.
    a. Rational0
    b. Thing
    c. Undefined
    d. Undefined

19. In mathematics, a _____ is any function which can be written as the ratio of two polynomial functions.

Chapter 4. Graphing and Optimization

    a. Thing
    b. Rational function0
    c. Undefined
    d. Undefined

20. A _____ is the part of a fraction that tells how many equal parts make up a whole, and which is used in the name of the fraction: "halves", "thirds", "fourths" or "quarters", "fifths" and so on.
    a. Concept
    b. Denominator0
    c. Undefined
    d. Undefined

21. The _____ integers are all the integers from zero on upwards.
    a. Nonnegative0
    b. Thing
    c. Undefined
    d. Undefined

22. A _____ fraction is a fraction in which the absolute value of the numerator is less than the denominator--hence, the absolute value of the fraction is less than 1.
    a. Proper0
    b. Thing
    c. Undefined
    d. Undefined

23. A _____ is a number that is less than zero.
    a. Negative number0
    b. Thing
    c. Undefined
    d. Undefined

24. In common philosophical language, a proposition or _____, is the content of an assertion, that is, it is true-or-false and defined by the meaning of a particular piece of language.
    a. Concept
    b. Statement0
    c. Undefined
    d. Undefined

25. _____ is a straight line or curve A to which another curve B the one being studied approaches closer and closer as one moves along it.
    a. Thing
    b. Vertical asymptote0
    c. Undefined
    d. Undefined

26. An _____ is a straight line or curve A to which another curve B approaches closer and closer as one moves along it. As one moves along B, the space between it and the _____ A becomes smaller and smaller, and can in fact be made as small as one could wish by going far enough along. A curve may or may not touch or cross its _____. In fact, the curve may intersect the _____ an infinite number of times.
    a. Asymptote0
    b. Thing
    c. Undefined
    d. Undefined

27. Deductive _____ is the kind of _____ in which the conclusion is necessitated by, or reached from, previously known facts (the premises).
    a. Thing
    b. Reasoning0
    c. Undefined
    d. Undefined

28. An _____ is a straight line around which a geometric figure can be rotated.

Chapter 4. Graphing and Optimization

   a. Axis0
   c. Undefined
   b. Thing
   d. Undefined

29. In mathematics, an _____ is a statement about the relative size or order of two objects.
   a. Thing
   c. Undefined
   b. Inequality0
   d. Undefined

30. A _____ is a numeral used to indicate a count. The most common use of the word today is to name the part of a fraction that tells the number or count of equal parts.
   a. Numerator0
   c. Undefined
   b. Thing
   d. Undefined

31. In mathematics, a _____ may be described informally as a number that can be given by an infinite decimal representation.
   a. Real number0
   c. Undefined
   b. Thing
   d. Undefined

32. Generally, a _____ is a splitting of something into parts.
   a. Thing
   c. Undefined
   b. Partition0
   d. Undefined

33. Mathematical _____ is used to represent ideas.
   a. Notation0
   c. Undefined
   b. Thing
   d. Undefined

34. Acid _____ ratio measures the ability of a company to use its near cash or quick assets to immediately extinguish its current liabilities.
   a. Test0
   c. Undefined
   b. Thing
   d. Undefined

35. _____ is the notation in which permitted values for a variable are expressed as ranging over a certain interval; "5 < x < 9" is an example of the application of _____.
   a. Interval notation0
   c. Undefined
   b. Thing
   d. Undefined

36. A _____ is a one-dimensional picture in which the integers are shown as specially-marked points evenly spaced on a line.
   a. Number line0
   c. Undefined
   b. Thing
   d. Undefined

37. A _____ is a special kind of ratio, indicating a relationship between two measurements with different units, such as miles to gallons or cents to pounds.
   a. Rate0
   c. Undefined
   b. Thing
   d. Undefined

38. In mathematics, a _____ is the result of multiplying, or an expression that identifies factors to be multiplied.

a. Product0
b. Thing
c. Undefined
d. Undefined

39. _____ is a form of periodic payment from an employer to an employee, which is specified in an employment contract.
   a. Gross pay0
   b. Thing
   c. Undefined
   d. Undefined

40. The payment of _____ as remuneration for services rendered or products sold is a common way to reward sales people.
   a. Thing
   b. Commission0
   c. Undefined
   d. Undefined

41. A _____ is a form of periodic payment from an employer to an employee, which is specified in an employment contract.
   a. Thing
   b. Salary0
   c. Undefined
   d. Undefined

42. _____ is often used to describe the measurement of the steepness, incline, gradient, or grade of a straight line. The _____ is defined as the ratio of the "rise" divided by the "run" between two points on a line, or in other words, the ratio of the altitude change to the horizontal distance between any two points on the line.
   a. Slope0
   b. Thing
   c. Undefined
   d. Undefined

43. in mathematics, maxima and minima, known collectively as _____, are the largest value maximum or smallest value minimum, that a function takes in a point either within a given neighborhood or on the function domain in its entirety global extremum.
   a. Extrema0
   b. Thing
   c. Undefined
   d. Undefined

44. The _____ is a measurement of how a function changes when the values of its inputs change.
   a. Derivative0
   b. Thing
   c. Undefined
   d. Undefined

45. There are two simple _____ the greatest common factor and least common multiple: standard factorization and prime factorization.
   a. Methods for finding0
   b. Thing
   c. Undefined
   d. Undefined

46. _____, from Latin meaning "to make progress", is defined in two different ways. Pure economic _____ is the increase in wealth that an investor has from making an investment, taking into consideration all costs associated with that investment including the opportunity cost of capital.
   a. Thing
   b. Profit0
   c. Undefined
   d. Undefined

Chapter 4. Graphing and Optimization

47. _____ is the application of tools and a processing medium to the transformation of raw materials into finished goods for sale.
   a. Thing
   b. Manufacturing0
   c. Undefined
   d. Undefined

48. In trigonometry, the _____ is a function defined as $\tan x = \sin x / \cos x$. The function is so-named because it can be defined as the length of a certain segment of a _____ (in the geometric sense) to the unit circle. In plane geometry, a line is _____ to a curve, at some point, if both line and curve pass through the point with the same direction.
   a. Tangent0
   b. Thing
   c. Undefined
   d. Undefined

49. In astronomy, geography, geometry and related sciences and contexts, a plane is said to be _____ at a given point if it is locally perpendicular to the gradient of the gravity field, i.e., with the direction of the gravitational force at that point.
   a. Horizontal0
   b. Thing
   c. Undefined
   d. Undefined

50. _____ has two distinct but etymologically-related meanings: one in geometry and one in trigonometry.
   a. Thing
   b. Tangent line0
   c. Undefined
   d. Undefined

51. _____ is an adjective usually refering to being in the centre.
   a. Central0
   b. Thing
   c. Undefined
   d. Undefined

52. Compass and straightedge or ruler-and-compass _____ is the _____ of lengths or angles using only an idealized ruler and compass.
   a. Thing
   b. Construction0
   c. Undefined
   d. Undefined

53. In mathematics, defined and _____ are used to explain whether or not expressions have meaningful, sensible, and unambiguous values.
   a. Thing
   b. Undefined0
   c. Undefined
   d. Undefined

54. In mathematics, a _____ of a k-place relation $L \subseteq X_1 \times ... \times X_k$ is one of the sets X_j, $1 \leq j \leq k$. In the special case where k = 2 and $L \subseteq X_1 \times X_2$ is a function $L : X_1 \to X_2$, it is conventional to refer to X_1 as the _____ of the function and to refer to X_2 as the codomain of the function.
   a. Thing
   b. Domain0
   c. Undefined
   d. Undefined

55. A _____ is a set whose members are members of another set or a set contained within another set.
   a. Thing
   b. Subset0
   c. Undefined
   d. Undefined

56. _____ are groups whose members are members of another set or a set contained within another set.

Chapter 4. Graphing and Optimization

a. Subsets0
b. Thing
c. Undefined
d. Undefined

57. A _____ is a function for which, intuitively, small changes in the input result in small changes in the output.
    a. Event
    b. Continuous function0
    c. Undefined
    d. Undefined

58. A real-valued function f defined on the real line is said to have a _____ point at the point x∗, if there exists some ε > 0, such that f when x − x∗ < ε.
    a. Local maximum0
    b. Thing
    c. Undefined
    d. Undefined

59. In mathematics, maxima and minima, known collectively as extrema, are the largest value maximum or smallest value minimum, that a function takes in a point either within a given neighborhood local _____ or on the function domain in its entirety global _____.
    a. Extremum0
    b. Thing
    c. Undefined
    d. Undefined

60. In mathematics, a _____ of a complex-valued function f is a member x of the domain of f such that f(x) vanishes at x, that is, x : f (x) = 0.
    a. Root0
    b. Thing
    c. Undefined
    d. Undefined

61. _____ is a free computer algebra system based on a 1982 version of Macsyma
    a. Thing
    b. Maxima0
    c. Undefined
    d. Undefined

62. _____ are points in the domain of a function at which the function takes a largest value or smallest value, either within a given neighborhood or on the function domain in its entirety.
    a. Thing
    b. Maxima and minima0
    c. Undefined
    d. Undefined

63. In mathematics, maxima and _____, known collectively as extrema, are points in the domain of a function at which the function takes a largest value .
    a. Minima0
    b. Thing
    c. Undefined
    d. Undefined

64. Any point where a graph makes contact with an coordinate axis is called an _____ of the graph
    a. Thing
    b. Intercept0
    c. Undefined
    d. Undefined

65. In banking and accountancy, the outstanding _____ is the amount of money owned, or due, that remains in a deposit account or a loan account at a given date, after all past remittances, payments and withdrawal have been accounted for.

Chapter 4. Graphing and Optimization

  a. Thing
  c. Undefined
  b. Balance0
  d. Undefined

66. _____ is the difference between the monetary value of exports and imports in an economy over a certain period of time.
  a. Trade balance0
  c. Undefined
  b. Thing
  d. Undefined

67. _____ is the extra revenue that an additional unit of product will bring a firm. It can also be described as the change in total revenue/change in number of units sold.
  a. Thing
  c. Undefined
  b. Marginal revenue0
  d. Undefined

68. _____ is a business term for the amount of money that a company receives from its activities in a given period, mostly from sales of products and/or services to customers
  a. Revenue0
  c. Undefined
  b. Thing
  d. Undefined

69. A _____ is a set of numbers that designate location in a given reference system, such as x,y in a planar _____ system or an x,y,z in a three-dimensional _____ system.
  a. Thing
  c. Undefined
  b. Coordinate0
  d. Undefined

70. In mathematics, an _____, mean, or central tendency of a data set refers to a measure of the "middle" or "expected" value of the data set.
  a. Average0
  c. Undefined
  b. Concept
  d. Undefined

71. _____ is the change in total cost that arises when the quantity produced changes by one unit.
  a. Marginal cost0
  c. Undefined
  b. Thing
  d. Undefined

72. _____ is the use of marginal concepts within economics. Marginal concepts include marginal cost, marginal productivity and marginal utility, the law of diminishing rates of substitution, and the law of diminishing marginal utility.
  a. Thing
  c. Undefined
  b. Marginal analysis0
  d. Undefined

73. The word _____ means curving in or hollowed inward.
  a. Concavity0
  c. Undefined
  b. Thing
  d. Undefined

74. _____ is a a point on a curve at which the tangent crosses the curve itself.
  a. Thing
  c. Undefined
  b. Inflection point0
  d. Undefined

75. In mathematics and its applications, a _____ is a system for assigning an n-tuple of numbers or scalars to each point in an n-dimensional space.
   a. Coordinate system0
   b. Concept
   c. Undefined
   d. Undefined

76. In mainstream economics, the word _____ refers to a general rise in prices measured against a standard level of purchasing power.
   a. Thing
   b. Inflation0
   c. Undefined
   d. Undefined

77. A _____ is an individual or household that purchases and uses goods and services generated within the economy.
   a. Consumer0
   b. Thing
   c. Undefined
   d. Undefined

78. _____ is a statistical time-series measure of a weighted average of prices of a specified set of goods and services purchased by consumers
   a. Thing
   b. Consumer price index0
   c. Undefined
   d. Undefined

79. The word _____ is used in a variety of ways in mathematics.
   a. Thing
   b. Index0
   c. Undefined
   d. Undefined

80. A _____ is a function that assigns a number to subsets of a given set.
   a. Measure0
   b. Thing
   c. Undefined
   d. Undefined

81. The _____ of measurement are a globally standardized and modernized form of the metric system.
   a. Thing
   b. Units0
   c. Undefined
   d. Undefined

82. In economics, supply and _____ describe market relations between prospective sellers and buyers of a good.
   a. Demand0
   b. Thing
   c. Undefined
   d. Undefined

83. _____ is a synonym for information.
   a. Thing
   b. Data0
   c. Undefined
   d. Undefined

84. _____ is a temperature scale named after the German physicist Daniel Gabriel _____ , who proposed it in 1724.
   a. Fahrenheit0
   b. Thing
   c. Undefined
   d. Undefined

85. In mathematics, there are several meanings of _____ depending on the subject.

Chapter 4. Graphing and Optimization

a. Thing
b. Degree0
c. Undefined
d. Undefined

86. An _____ or member of a set is an object that when collected together make up the set.
    a. Element0
    b. Thing
    c. Undefined
    d. Undefined

87. _____ is the state of being greater than any finite number, however large.
    a. Thing
    b. Infinity0
    c. Undefined
    d. Undefined

88. In mathematics, especially in order theory, an _____ of a subset S of some partially ordered set is an element of P which is greater than or equal to every element of S.
    a. Upper bound0
    b. Thing
    c. Undefined
    d. Undefined

89. In mathematics, the multiplicative inverse of a number x, denoted 1/x or x^{-1}, is the number which, when multiplied by x, yields 1. The multiplicative inverse of x is also called the _____ of x.
    a. Reciprocal0
    b. Thing
    c. Undefined
    d. Undefined

90. In mathematics, the _____ (or modulus) of a real number is its numerical value without regard to its sign.
    a. Thing
    b. Absolute value0
    c. Undefined
    d. Undefined

91. _____ has many meanings, most of which simply .
    a. Thing
    b. Power0
    c. Undefined
    d. Undefined

92. A _____ is a quantity that denotes the proportional amount or magnitude of one quantity relative to another.
    a. Thing
    b. Ratio0
    c. Undefined
    d. Undefined

93. In mathematics, the concept of a _____ tries to capture the intuitive idea of a geometrical one-dimensional and continuous object. A simple example is the circle.
    a. Thing
    b. Curve0
    c. Undefined
    d. Undefined

94. Graphing on a Cartesian plane is sometimes referred to as _____.
    a. Thing
    b. Curve sketching0
    c. Undefined
    d. Undefined

95. In calculus and other branches of mathematical analysis, an _____ is an algebraic expression obtained in the context of limits.

Chapter 4. Graphing and Optimization

    a. Indeterminate form0   b. Thing
    c. Undefined   d. Undefined

96. In mathematics, _____ is the decomposition of an object into a product of other objects, or factors, which when multiplied together give the original.
    a. Thing   b. Factoring0
    c. Undefined   d. Undefined

97. In geometry, an _____ angle is an angle that is not a 90 degree angle, or an angle that is divisible by 90: 180, 270, 360/0
    a. Oblique0   b. Thing
    c. Undefined   d. Undefined

98. A _____ signifies a point or points of probability on a subject e.g., the _____ of creativity, which allows for the formation of rule or norm or law by interpretation of the phenomena events that can be created.
    a. Principle0   b. Thing
    c. Undefined   d. Undefined

99. The word _____ comes from the Latin word linearis, which means created by lines.
    a. Thing   b. Linear0
    c. Undefined   d. Undefined

100. Initial objects are also called _____, and terminal objects are also called final.
    a. Thing   b. Coterminal0
    c. Undefined   d. Undefined

101. An _____ is a combination of numbers, operators, grouping symbols and/or free variables and bound variables arranged in a meaningful way which can be evaluated..
    a. Thing   b. Expression0
    c. Undefined   d. Undefined

102. In plane geometry, a _____ is a polygon with four equal sides, four right angles, and parallel opposite sides. In algebra, the _____ of a number is that number multiplied by itself.
    a. Square0   b. Thing
    c. Undefined   d. Undefined

103. An _____ is when two lines intersect somewhere on a plane creating a right angle at intersection
    a. Axes0   b. Thing
    c. Undefined   d. Undefined

104. In the scientific method, an _____ (Latin: ex-+-periri, "of (or from) trying"), is a set of actions and observations, performed in the context of solving a particular problem or question, in order to support or falsify a hypothesis or research concerning phenomena.
    a. Experiment0   b. Thing
    c. Undefined   d. Undefined

Chapter 4. Graphing and Optimization

105. A _____ is 360° or 2δ radians.
   a. Turn0
   b. Thing
   c. Undefined
   d. Undefined

106. _____ are objects, characters, or other concrete representations of ideas, concepts, or other abstractions.
   a. Symbols0
   b. Thing
   c. Undefined
   d. Undefined

107. The term _____ refers to the largest and the smallest element of a set.
   a. Extreme value0
   b. Thing
   c. Undefined
   d. Undefined

108. A _____ is a negotiable instrument instructing a financial institution to pay a specific amount of a specific currency from a specific demand account held in the maker/depositor's name with that institution. Both the maker and payee may be natural persons or legal entities.
   a. Thing
   b. Check0
   c. Undefined
   d. Undefined

109. A _____ is a symbolic representation denoting a quantity or expression. It often represents an "unknown" quantity that has the potential to change.
   a. Variable0
   b. Thing
   c. Undefined
   d. Undefined

110. A _____ is an abstract model that uses mathematical language to describe the behavior of a system. Eykhoff defined a _____ as 'a representation of the essential aspects of an existing system which presents knowledge of that system in usable form'.
   a. Thing
   b. Mathematical model0
   c. Undefined
   d. Undefined

111. In mathematics and logic, a _____ proof is a way of showing the truth or falsehood of a given statement by a straightforward combination of established facts, usually existing lemmas and theorems, without making any further assumptions.
   a. Direct0
   b. Thing
   c. Undefined
   d. Undefined

112. A _____ is the result of the addition of a set of numbers. The numbers may be natural numbers, complex numbers, matrices, or still more complicated objects. An infinite _____ is a subtle procedure known as a series.
   a. Thing
   b. Sum0
   c. Undefined
   d. Undefined

113. In geometry, a _____ is defined as a quadrilateral where all four of its angles are right angles.
   a. Thing
   b. Rectangle0
   c. Undefined
   d. Undefined

114. _____ is the distance around a given two-dimensional object. As a general rule, the _____ of a polygon can always be calculated by adding all the length of the sides together. So, the formula for triangles is P = a + b + c, where a, b and c stand for each side of it. For quadrilaterals the equation is P = a + b + c + d. For equilateral polygons, P = na, where n is the number of sides and a is the side length.
  a. Perimeter0
  b. Thing
  c. Undefined
  d. Undefined

115. In logic and mathematics, logical _____ is a logical relation that holds between a set T of formulas and a formula B when every model (or interpretation or valuation) of T is also a model of B.
  a. Implication0
  b. Concept
  c. Undefined
  d. Undefined

116. _____ is a kind of property which exists as magnitude or multitude. It is among the basic classes of things along with quality, substance, change, and relation.
  a. Thing
  b. Amount0
  c. Undefined
  d. Undefined

117. In mathematics, an _____ is any of the arguments, i.e. "inputs", to a function. Thus if we have a function f(x), then x is a _____.
  a. Independent variable0
  b. Thing
  c. Undefined
  d. Undefined

118. _____ is a regression method that models the relationship between a dependent variable Y, independent variables Xp, and a random term å.
  a. Thing
  b. Linear regression0
  c. Undefined
  d. Undefined

119. _____ is the ability to hold, receive or absorb, or a measure thereof, similar to the concept of volume.
  a. Capacity0
  b. Concept
  c. Undefined
  d. Undefined

120. The _____ of a solid object is the three-dimensional concept of how much space it occupies, often quantified numerically.
  a. Volume0
  b. Thing
  c. Undefined
  d. Undefined

121. In classical geometry, a _____ of a circle or sphere is any line segment from its center to its boundary. By extension, the _____ of a circle or sphere is the length of any such segment. The _____ is half the diameter. In science and engineering the term _____ of curvature is commonly used as a synonym for _____.
  a. Radius0
  b. Thing
  c. Undefined
  d. Undefined

122. In geometry, _____ angles are angles that have a common ray coming out of the vertex going between two other rays.

Chapter 4. Graphing and Optimization

a. Adjacent0
b. Concept
c. Undefined
d. Undefined

123. A _____ is a unit of length, usually used to measure distance, in a number of different systems, including Imperial units, United States customary units and Norwegian/Swedish mil. Its size can vary from system to system, but in each is between 1 and 10 kilometers. In contemporary English contexts _____ refers to either:
a. Mile0
b. Thing
c. Undefined
d. Undefined

124. _____ is a unit of speed, expressing the number of international miles covered per hour.
a. Miles per hour0
b. Thing
c. Undefined
d. Undefined

125. In mathematics, a _____ is a quadric surface, with the following equation in Cartesian coordinates: $(x/_a)^2 + (y/_b)^2 = 1$.
a. Thing
b. Cylinder0
c. Undefined
d. Undefined

126. _____ is the process in which two clone daughter cells are produced by the cell division of one bacterium.
a. Bacteria growth0
b. Thing
c. Undefined
d. Undefined

127. A _____ is a fee added to a customer's bill.
a. Thing
b. Service charge0
c. Undefined
d. Undefined

128. In sociology and biology a _____ is the collection of people or organisms of a particular species living in a given geographic area or space, usually measured by a census.
a. Population0
b. Thing
c. Undefined
d. Undefined

129. _____, in economics and political economy, are the distributions or payments awarded to the various suppliers of the factors of production.
a. Returns0
b. Thing
c. Undefined
d. Undefined

130. According to _____ relationship, in a production system with fixed and variable inputs, beyond some point, each additional unit of variable input yields less and less additional output.
a. Thing
b. Diminishing returns0
c. Undefined
d. Undefined

131. _____ are citizens in a democratic form of governance that have checked in with some form of a central registry, which in turn permits them to vote.
a. Registered voters0
b. Thing
c. Undefined
d. Undefined

132. _____ are procedures that allow people to exchange information by one of several methods.
a. Communications0
b. Thing
c. Undefined
d. Undefined

133. In mathematics, two quantities are called _____ if they vary in such a way that one of the quantities is a constant multiple of the other, or equivalently if they have a constant ratio.
a. Proportional0
b. Thing
c. Undefined
d. Undefined

Chapter 5. Additional Derivative Topics

1. A _____ function is a function for which, intuitively, small changes in the input result in small changes in the output.
   - a. Event
   - b. Continuous0
   - c. Undefined
   - d. Undefined

2. In mathematics, _____ growth occurs when the growth rate of a function is always proportional to the function's current size.
   - a. Exponential0
   - b. Thing
   - c. Undefined
   - d. Undefined

3. _____ is one of the most important functions in mathematics. A function commonly used to study growth and decay
   - a. Thing
   - b. Exponential function0
   - c. Undefined
   - d. Undefined

4. _____ is the fee paid on borrowed money.
   - a. Interest0
   - b. Thing
   - c. Undefined
   - d. Undefined

5. _____ interest refers to the fact that whenever interest is calculated, it is based not only on the original principal, but also on any unpaid interest that has been added to the principal.
   - a. Thing
   - b. Compound0
   - c. Undefined
   - d. Undefined

6. _____ refers to the fact that whenever interest is calculated, it is based not only on the original principal, but also on any unpaid interest that has been added to the principal. The more frequently interest is compounded, the faster the balance grows.
   - a. Compound interest0
   - b. Concept
   - c. Undefined
   - d. Undefined

7. In mathematics and the mathematical sciences, a _____ is a fixed, but possibly unspecified, value. This is in contrast to a variable, which is not fixed.
   - a. Thing
   - b. Constant0
   - c. Undefined
   - d. Undefined

8. The mathematical concept of a _____ expresses the intuitive idea of deterministic dependence between two quantities, one of which is viewed as primary and the other as secondary. A _____ then is a way to associate a unique output for each input of a specified type, for example, a real number or an element of a given set.
   - a. Thing
   - b. Function0
   - c. Undefined
   - d. Undefined

9. In mathematics, an _____ number is any real number that is not a rational number- that is, it is a number which cannot be expressed as a fraction m/n, where m and n are integers.
   - a. Irrational0
   - b. Thing
   - c. Undefined
   - d. Undefined

10. In mathematics, an _____ is any real number that is not a rational number ¡ª that is, it is a number which cannot be expressed as m/n, where m and n are integers.

a. Irrational number0
b. Thing
c. Undefined
d. Undefined

11. _____, a field in mathematics, is the study of how functions change when their inputs change. The primary object of study in _____ is the derivative.
   a. Thing
   b. Differential calculus0
   c. Undefined
   d. Undefined

12. In mathematics, a _____ is a demonstration that, assuming certain axioms, some statement is necessarily true.
   a. Thing
   b. Proof0
   c. Undefined
   d. Undefined

13. _____ has many meanings, most of which simply .
   a. Power0
   b. Thing
   c. Undefined
   d. Undefined

14. Leonhard _____ was a pioneering Swiss mathematician and physicist, who spent most of his life in Russia and Germany.
   a. Euler0
   b. Person
   c. Undefined
   d. Undefined

15. _____ was a pioneering Swiss mathematician and physicist, who spent most of his life in Russia and Germany.
   a. Person
   b. Leonhard Euler0
   c. Undefined
   d. Undefined

16. A _____ is a special kind of ratio, indicating a relationship between two measurements with different units, such as miles to gallons or cents to pounds.
   a. Thing
   b. Rate0
   c. Undefined
   d. Undefined

17. _____ is a kind of property which exists as magnitude or multitude. It is among the basic classes of things along with quality, substance, change, and relation.
   a. Thing
   b. Amount0
   c. Undefined
   d. Undefined

18. Equivalence is the condition of being _____ or essentially equal.
   a. Thing
   b. Equivalent0
   c. Undefined
   d. Undefined

19. An _____ is a combination of numbers, operators, grouping symbols and/or free variables and bound variables arranged in a meaningful way which can be evaluated..
   a. Expression0
   b. Thing
   c. Undefined
   d. Undefined

20. An _____ is the fee paid on borrow money.

Chapter 5. Additional Derivative Topics

a. Interest rate0
b. Concept
c. Undefined
d. Undefined

21. In business, particularly accounting, a _____ is the time intervals that the accounts, statement, payments, or other calculations cover.
   a. Thing
   b. Period0
   c. Undefined
   d. Undefined

22. A _____ is 360° or 2∂ radians.
   a. Turn0
   b. Thing
   c. Undefined
   d. Undefined

23. In mathematics, a _____ may be described informally as a number that can be given by an infinite decimal representation.
   a. Thing
   b. Real number0
   c. Undefined
   d. Undefined

24. _____ or investing is a term with several closely-related meanings in business management, finance and economics, related to saving or deferring consumption.
   a. Thing
   b. Investment0
   c. Undefined
   d. Undefined

25. _____ generally derives from name. A _____ quantity e.g., length, diameter, volume, voltage, value is generally the quantity according to which some item has been named or is generally referred to.
   a. Nominal0
   b. Thing
   c. Undefined
   d. Undefined

26. The _____, the average in everyday English, which is also called the arithmetic _____ (and is distinguished from the geometric _____ or harmonic _____). The average is also called the sample _____. The expected value of a random variable, which is also called the population _____.
   a. Mean0
   b. Thing
   c. Undefined
   d. Undefined

27. _____ is the logarithm to the base e, where e is an irrational constant approximately equal to 2.718281828459.
   a. Natural logarithm0
   b. Thing
   c. Undefined
   d. Undefined

28. In mathematics, a _____ of a number x is the exponent y of the power by such that $x = b^y$. The value used for the base b must be neither 0 nor 1, nor a root of 1 in the case of the extension to complex numbers, and is typically 10, e, or 2.
   a. Logarithm0
   b. Thing
   c. Undefined
   d. Undefined

29. In mathematics, an _____ is a statement about the relative size or order of two objects.
   a. Thing
   b. Inequality0
   c. Undefined
   d. Undefined

Chapter 5. Additional Derivative Topics

30. _____ of a single or multiple future payments is the nominal amounts of money to change hands at some future date, discounted to account for the time value of money, and other factors such as investment risk.
    a. Present value0
    b. Thing
    c. Undefined
    d. Undefined

31. The _____ is the period of time required for a quantity to double in size or value.
    a. Doubling time0
    b. Thing
    c. Undefined
    d. Undefined

32. The _____ is a measurement of how a function changes when the values of its inputs change.
    a. Thing
    b. Derivative0
    c. Undefined
    d. Undefined

33. _____ is the process in which an unstable atomic nucleus loses energy by emitting radiation in the form of particles or electromagnetic waves.
    a. Radioactive decay0
    b. Thing
    c. Undefined
    d. Undefined

34. The _____ is the total number of human beings alive on the planet Earth at a given time.
    a. World population0
    b. Thing
    c. Undefined
    d. Undefined

35. In sociology and biology a _____ is the collection of people or organisms of a particular species living in a given geographic area or space, usually measured by a census.
    a. Thing
    b. Population0
    c. Undefined
    d. Undefined

36. A _____ is an abstract model that uses mathematical language to describe the behavior of a system. Eykhoff defined a _____ as 'a representation of the essential aspects of an existing system which presents knowledge of that system in usable form'.
    a. Mathematical model0
    b. Thing
    c. Undefined
    d. Undefined

37. _____ is change in population over time, and can be quantified as the change in the number of individuals in a population per unit time.
    a. Thing
    b. Population growth0
    c. Undefined
    d. Undefined

38. A _____ is a symbolic representation denoting a quantity or expression. It often represents an "unknown" quantity that has the potential to change.
    a. Variable0
    b. Thing
    c. Undefined
    d. Undefined

39. _____ is a method for differentiating expressions involving exponentiation the power operation.

Chapter 5. Additional Derivative Topics

a. Power rule0
b. Thing
c. Undefined
d. Undefined

40. _____ is a straight line or curve A to which another curve B the one being studied approaches closer and closer as one moves along it.
   a. Vertical asymptote0
   b. Thing
   c. Undefined
   d. Undefined

41. _____ are the basic objects of study in graph theory. Informally speaking, a graph is a set of objects called points, nodes, or vertices connected by links called lines or edges.
   a. Graphs0
   b. Thing
   c. Undefined
   d. Undefined

42. An _____ is a straight line or curve A to which another curve B approaches closer and closer as one moves along it. As one moves along B, the space between it and the _____ A becomes smaller and smaller, and can in fact be made as small as one could wish by going far enough along. A curve may or may not touch or cross its _____. In fact, the curve may intersect the _____ an infinite number of times.
   a. Asymptote0
   b. Thing
   c. Undefined
   d. Undefined

43. An _____ is a straight line around which a geometric figure can be rotated.
   a. Thing
   b. Axis0
   c. Undefined
   d. Undefined

44. In astronomy, geography, geometry and related sciences and contexts, a plane is said to be _____ at a given point if it is locally perpendicular to the gradient of the gravity field, i.e., with the direction of the gravitational force at that point.
   a. Thing
   b. Horizontal0
   c. Undefined
   d. Undefined

45. Any point where a graph makes contact with an coordinate axis is called an _____ of the graph
   a. Intercept0
   b. Thing
   c. Undefined
   d. Undefined

46. In mathematics, a _____ of a k-place relation $L \subseteq X_1 \times ... \times X_k$ is one of the sets X_j, $1 \leq j \leq k$. In the special case where k = 2 and $L \subseteq X_1 \times X_2$ is a function $L : X_1 \rightarrow X_2$, it is conventional to refer to X_1 as the _____ of the function and to refer to X_2 as the codomain of the function.
   a. Domain0
   b. Thing
   c. Undefined
   d. Undefined

47. Generally, a _____ is a splitting of something into parts.
   a. Partition0
   b. Thing
   c. Undefined
   d. Undefined

48. _____, from Latin meaning "to make progress", is defined in two different ways. Pure economic _____ is the increase in wealth that an investor has from making an investment, taking into consideration all costs associated with that investment including the opportunity cost of capital.

a. Thing
b. Profit0
c. Undefined
d. Undefined

49. Acid _____ ratio measures the ability of a company to use its near cash or quick assets to immediately extinguish its current liabilities.
a. Test0
b. Thing
c. Undefined
d. Undefined

50. A _____ is a negotiable instrument instructing a financial institution to pay a specific amount of a specific currency from a specific demand account held in the maker/depositor's name with that institution. Both the maker and payee may be natural persons or legal entities.
a. Thing
b. Check0
c. Undefined
d. Undefined

51. In trigonometry, the _____ is a function defined as $\tan x = \sin x / \cos x$. The function is so-named because it can be defined as the length of a certain segment of a _____ (in the geometric sense) to the unit circle. In plane geometry, a line is _____ to a curve, at some point, if both line and curve pass through the point with the same direction.
a. Thing
b. Tangent0
c. Undefined
d. Undefined

52. in mathematics, maxima and minima, known collectively as _____, are the largest value maximum or smallest value minimum, that a function takes in a point either within a given neighborhood or on the function domain in its entirety global extremum.
a. Extrema0
b. Thing
c. Undefined
d. Undefined

53. In elementary algebra, an _____ is a set that contains every real number between two indicated numbers and may contain the two numbers themselves.
a. Thing
b. Interval0
c. Undefined
d. Undefined

54. In mathematics, an inequality is a statement about the relative size or order of two objects. For example 14 > 10, or 14 is _____ 10.
a. Greater than0
b. Thing
c. Undefined
d. Undefined

55. In mathematics, the _____ of two sets A and B is the set that contains all elements of A that also belong to B (or equivalently, all elements of B that also belong to A), but no other elements.
a. Thing
b. Intersection0
c. Undefined
d. Undefined

56. In probability theory, _____ are various sets of outcomes (a subset of the sample space) to which a probability is assigned.
a. Thing
b. Events0
c. Undefined
d. Undefined

Chapter 5. Additional Derivative Topics

57. In economics, supply and _____ describe market relations between prospective sellers and buyers of a good.
   a. Demand0
   b. Thing
   c. Undefined
   d. Undefined

58. In mathematics, an _____, mean, or central tendency of a data set refers to a measure of the "middle" or "expected" value of the data set.
   a. Concept
   b. Average0
   c. Undefined
   d. Undefined

59. In mathematics, a _____ is the result of multiplying, or an expression that identifies factors to be multiplied.
   a. Product0
   b. Thing
   c. Undefined
   d. Undefined

60. The _____ of measurement are a globally standardized and modernized form of the metric system.
   a. Units0
   b. Thing
   c. Undefined
   d. Undefined

61. _____ is a business term for the amount of money that a company receives from its activities in a given period, mostly from sales of products and/or services to customers
   a. Revenue0
   b. Thing
   c. Undefined
   d. Undefined

62. In the scientific method, an _____ (Latin: ex-+-periri, "of (or from) trying"), is a set of actions and observations, performed in the context of solving a particular problem or question, in order to support or falsify a hypothesis or research concerning phenomena.
   a. Thing
   b. Experiment0
   c. Undefined
   d. Undefined

63. In calculus, the _____ is a formula for the derivative of the composite of two functions.
   a. Concept
   b. Chain rule0
   c. Undefined
   d. Undefined

64. A _____ number is a positive integer which has a positive divisor other than one or itself.
   a. Composite0
   b. ThIng
   c. Undefined
   d. Undefined

65. A _____, formed by the composition of one function on another, represents the application of the former to the result of the application of the latter to the argument of the composite.
   a. Thing
   b. Composite function0
   c. Undefined
   d. Undefined

66. One of the three formats applicable to a quadratic function is the _____ which is defined as $f = ax^2 + bx + c$.
   a. General form0
   b. Thing
   c. Undefined
   d. Undefined

67. In mathematics, a _____ of a positive integer n is a way of writing n as a sum of positive integers.

| a. Thing | b. Composition0 |
| c. Undefined | d. Undefined |

68. In mathematics, a _____ is an expression that is constructed from one or more variables and constants, using only the operations of addition, subtraction, multiplication, and constant positive whole number exponents. is a _____. Note in particular that division by an expression containing a variable is not in general allowed in polynomials. [1]

| a. Polynomial0 | b. Thing |
| c. Undefined | d. Undefined |

69. Fixed costs are expenses whose total does not change in proportion to the activity of a business.Unit fixed costs decline with volume following a retangular hyperbola as the volume of production.Variable costs by contrast change in relation to the activity of a business such as sales or production volume.Along with variable costs,fixed costs make up one of the two components of total cost. In the most simple production function total cost is equal to fixed costs plus variable costs.In accounting terminology, fixed costs will broadly include all costs which are not included in cost of goods sold, and variable costs are those captured in costs of goods sold. The implicit assumption required to make the equivalence between the accounting and economics terminology is that the accounting period is equal to the period in which fixed costs do not vary in relation to production. In practice, this equivalence does not always hold and depending on the period under consideration by management, some overhead expenses can be adjusted by management, and the specific allocation of each expense to each category will be decided under cost accounting.In business planning and management accounting, usage of the terms fixed costs, variable costs and others will often differ from usage in economics, and may depend on the intended use. For example, costs may be segregated into per unit costs fixed costs per period, and variable costs as a proportion of revenue. Capital expenditures will usually be allocated separately, and depending on the purpose, a portion may be regularly allocated to expenses as depreciation and amortization and seen as a _____ per period, or the entire amount may be considered upfront fixed costs.

| a. Fixed cost0 | b. Thing |
| c. Undefined | d. Undefined |

70. In mathematics, a subset of Euclidean space R^n is called _____ if it is closed and bounded.

| a. Compact0 | b. Thing |
| c. Undefined | d. Undefined |

71. _____ is a special mathematical relationship between two quantities.Two quantities are called proportional if they vary in such a way that one of the quantities is a constant multiple of the other, or equivalently if they have a constant ratio.

| a. Proportionality0 | b. Thing |
| c. Undefined | d. Undefined |

72. A central concept in science and the scientific method is that all evidence must be _____, or empirically based, that is, dependent on evidence or consequences that are observable by the senses.

| a. Empirical0 | b. Thing |
| c. Undefined | d. Undefined |

73. _____ is a synonym for information.

| a. Data0 | b. Thing |
| c. Undefined | d. Undefined |

Chapter 5. Additional Derivative Topics

74. _____ is process in which two clone daughter cells are produced by the cell division of one bacterium.
    a. Bacterial growth0
    b. Thing
    c. Undefined
    d. Undefined

75. _____, in a human resources context refers to the characteristic of a given company or industry, relative to rate at which an employer gains and loses staff.
    a. Thing
    b. Turnover0
    c. Undefined
    d. Undefined

76. Mathematical _____ is used to represent ideas.
    a. Thing
    b. Notation0
    c. Undefined
    d. Undefined

77. _____ is to give an equation R(x,y) = S(x,y) that at least in part has the same graph as y = f(x).
    a. Thing
    b. Implicit differentiation0
    c. Undefined
    d. Undefined

78. In mathematics, an _____ is any of the arguments, i.e. "inputs", to a function. Thus if we have a function f(x), then x is a _____.
    a. Independent variable0
    b. Thing
    c. Undefined
    d. Undefined

79. In a function the _____, is the variable which is the value, i.e. the "output", of the function.
    a. Thing
    b. Dependent variable0
    c. Undefined
    d. Undefined

80. _____ are objects, characters, or other concrete representations of ideas, concepts, or other abstractions.
    a. Thing
    b. Symbols0
    c. Undefined
    d. Undefined

81. In mathematics and logic, a _____ proof is a way of showing the truth or falsehood of a given statement by a straightforward combination of established facts, usually existing lemmas and theorems, without making any further assumptions.
    a. Direct0
    b. ThIng
    c. Undefined
    d. Undefined

82. In mathematics, the _____ f is the collection of all ordered pairs . In particular, graph means the graphical representation of this collection, in the form of a curve or surface, together with axes, etc. Graphing on a Cartesian plane is sometimes referred to as curve sketching.
    a. Graph of a function0
    b. Thing
    c. Undefined
    d. Undefined

83. _____ is often used to describe the measurement of the steepness, incline, gradient, or grade of a straight line. The _____ is defined as the ratio of the "rise" divided by the "run" between two points on a line, or in other words, the ratio of the altitude change to the horizontal distance between any two points on the line.

a. Slope0
b. Thing
c. Undefined
d. Undefined

84. _____ has two distinct but etymologically-related meanings: one in geometry and one in trigonometry.
   a. Tangent line0
   b. Thing
   c. Undefined
   d. Undefined

85. The act of _____ is the calculated approximation of a result which is usable even if input data may be incomplete, uncertain, or noisy.
   a. Estimating0
   b. Thing
   c. Undefined
   d. Undefined

86. _____ of an object is its speed in a particular direction.
   a. Thing
   b. Velocity0
   c. Undefined
   d. Undefined

87. In set theory and other branches of mathematics, the _____ of a collection of sets is the set that contains everything that belongs to any of the sets, but nothing else.
   a. Thing
   b. Union0
   c. Undefined
   d. Undefined

88. A _____ is a compensation which workers receive in exchange for their labor.
   a. Thing
   b. Wage0
   c. Undefined
   d. Undefined

89. In economics _____ means before deductions brutto, e.g. _____ domestic or national product, or _____ profit or income
   a. Thing
   b. Gross0
   c. Undefined
   d. Undefined

90. In differential calculus, _____ problems involve finding the rate at which a quantity is changing by relating that quantity to other quantities whose rates of change are known.
   a. Thing
   b. Related rates0
   c. Undefined
   d. Undefined

91. A _____ is a unit of length, usually used to measure distance, in a number of different systems, including Imperial units, United States customary units and Norwegian/Swedish mil. Its size can vary from system to system, but in each is between 1 and 10 kilometers. In contemporary English contexts _____ refers to either:
   a. Thing
   b. Mile0
   c. Undefined
   d. Undefined

92. _____ is a unit of speed, expressing the number of international miles covered per hour.
   a. Miles per hour0
   b. Thing
   c. Undefined
   d. Undefined

Chapter 5. Additional Derivative Topics

93. A _____ is a set of numbers that designate location in a given reference system, such as x,y in a planar _____ system or an x,y,z in a three-dimensional _____ system.
    a. Thing
    b. Coordinate0
    c. Undefined
    d. Undefined

94. In classical geometry, a _____ of a circle or sphere is any line segment from its center to its boundary. By extension, the _____ of a circle or sphere is the length of any such segment. The _____ is half the diameter. In science and engineering the term _____ of curvature is commonly used as a synonym for _____.
    a. Thing
    b. Radius0
    c. Undefined
    d. Undefined

95. The _____ of a solid object is the three-dimensional concept of how much space it occupies, often quantified numerically.
    a. Thing
    b. Volume0
    c. Undefined
    d. Undefined

96. _____ is a physical property of a system that underlies the common notions of hot and cold; something that is hotter has the greater _____.
    a. Temperature0
    b. Thing
    c. Undefined
    d. Undefined

97. The _____ rule, also known as a slipstick, is a mechanical analog computer, consisting of at least two finely divided scales , most often a fixed outer pair and a movable inner one, with a sliding window called the cursor.
    a. Slide0
    b. Thing
    c. Undefined
    d. Undefined

98. A _____ is one of the basic shapes of geometry: a polygon with three vertices and three sides which are straight line segments.
    a. Thing
    b. Triangle0
    c. Undefined
    d. Undefined

99. _____ is a relation in Euclidean geometry among the three sides of a right triangle.
    a. Pythagorean Theorem0
    b. Thing
    c. Undefined
    d. Undefined

100. The _____ of a right triangle is the triangle's longest side; the side opposite the right angle.
    a. Hypotenuse0
    b. Thing
    c. Undefined
    d. Undefined

101. _____ has one 90° internal angle a right angle.
    a. Right triangle0
    b. Thing
    c. Undefined
    d. Undefined

102. In mathematics, a _____ is a statement that can be proved on the basis of explicitly stated or previously agreed assumptions.

a. Thing
b. Theorem0
c. Undefined
d. Undefined

103. The metre (or _____, see spelling differences) is a measure of length. It is the basic unit of length in the metric system and in the International System of Units (SI), used around the world for general and scientific purposes.
   a. Concept
   b. Meter0
   c. Undefined
   d. Undefined

104. _____ are a measure of time.
   a. Minutes0
   b. Thing
   c. Undefined
   d. Undefined

105. In plane geometry, a _____ is a polygon with four equal sides, four right angles, and parallel opposite sides. In algebra, the _____ of a number is that number multiplied by itself.
   a. Square0
   b. Thing
   c. Undefined
   d. Undefined

106. _____ is the use of marginal concepts within economics. Marginal concepts include marginal cost, marginal productivity and marginal utility, the law of diminishing rates of substitution, and the law of diminishing marginal utility.
   a. Thing
   b. Marginal analysis0
   c. Undefined
   d. Undefined

107. _____ is the application of tools and a processing medium to the transformation of raw materials into finished goods for sale.
   a. Thing
   b. Manufacturing0
   c. Undefined
   d. Undefined

108. In economics and business studies, the _____ is an elasticity that measures the nature and degree of the relationship between changes in quantity demanded of a good and changes in its price.
   a. Thing
   b. Elasticity of demand0
   c. Undefined
   d. Undefined

109. A _____ is a function that assigns a number to subsets of a given set.
   a. Measure0
   b. Thing
   c. Undefined
   d. Undefined

110. _____, in economics and political economy, are the distributions or payments awarded to the various suppliers of the factors of production.
   a. Thing
   b. Returns0
   c. Undefined
   d. Undefined

111. According to _____ relationship, in a production system with fixed and variable inputs, beyond some point, each additional unit of variable input yields less and less additional output.
   a. Thing
   b. Diminishing returns0
   c. Undefined
   d. Undefined

Chapter 5. Additional Derivative Topics

112. _____ is the ability to hold, receive or absorb, or a measure thereof, similar to the concept of volume.
a. Capacity0
b. Concept
c. Undefined
d. Undefined

113. _____ usually refers to the biological _____ of a population level that can be supported for an organism, given the quantity of food, habitat, water and other life infrastructure present.
a. Thing
b. Carrying capacity0
c. Undefined
d. Undefined

Chapter 6. Integration

1. _____ is an extension of the concept of a sum.
   - a. Thing
   - b. Definite integral0
   - c. Undefined
   - d. Undefined

2. The _____ of a function is an extension of the concept of a sum, and are identified or found through the use of integration.
   - a. Integral0
   - b. Thing
   - c. Undefined
   - d. Undefined

3. An _____ of a function f is a function F whose derivative is equal to f, i.e., F' = f.
   - a. Antiderivative0
   - b. Thing
   - c. Undefined
   - d. Undefined

4. In mathematics, _____ is an elementary arithmetic operation. When one of the numbers is a whole number, _____ is the repeated sum of the other number.
   - a. Thing
   - b. Multiplication0
   - c. Undefined
   - d. Undefined

5. In mathematics, _____ growth occurs when the growth rate of a function is always proportional to the function's current size.
   - a. Exponential0
   - b. Thing
   - c. Undefined
   - d. Undefined

6. In mathematics, a _____ of a complex-valued function f is a member x of the domain of f such that f(x) vanishes at x, that is, x : f (x) = 0.
   - a. Thing
   - b. Root0
   - c. Undefined
   - d. Undefined

7. _____ has many meanings, most of which simply .
   - a. Thing
   - b. Power0
   - c. Undefined
   - d. Undefined

8. The _____ is a measurement of how a function changes when the values of its inputs change.
   - a. Thing
   - b. Derivative0
   - c. Undefined
   - d. Undefined

9. The mathematical concept of a _____ expresses the intuitive idea of deterministic dependence between two quantities, one of which is viewed as primary and the other as secondary. A _____ then is a way to associate a unique output for each input of a specified type, for example, a real number or an element of a given set.
   - a. Thing
   - b. Function0
   - c. Undefined
   - d. Undefined

10. In mathematics, a _____ is a demonstration that, assuming certain axioms, some statement is necessarily true.
    - a. Proof0
    - b. Thing
    - c. Undefined
    - d. Undefined

11. In mathematics, a _____ is a statement that can be proved on the basis of explicitly stated or previously agreed assumptions.
  a. Thing
  b. Theorem0
  c. Undefined
  d. Undefined

12. In mathematics, a _____ may be described informally as a number that can be given by an infinite decimal representation.
  a. Real number0
  b. Thing
  c. Undefined
  d. Undefined

13. An _____ is a combination of numbers, operators, grouping symbols and/or free variables and bound variables arranged in a meaningful way which can be evaluated..
  a. Thing
  b. Expression0
  c. Undefined
  d. Undefined

14. In mathematics and the mathematical sciences, a _____ is a fixed, but possibly unspecified, value. This is in contrast to a variable, which is not fixed.
  a. Constant0
  b. Thing
  c. Undefined
  d. Undefined

15. In elementary algebra, an _____ is a set that contains every real number between two indicated numbers and may contain the two numbers themselves.
  a. Thing
  b. Interval0
  c. Undefined
  d. Undefined

16. A _____ is a symbolic representation denoting a quantity or expression. It often represents an "unknown" quantity that has the potential to change.
  a. Variable0
  b. Thing
  c. Undefined
  d. Undefined

17. _____ in calculus is primitive or indefinite integral of a function f is a function F whose derivative is equal to f, i.e., F Œ = f. The process of solving for antiderivatives is _____
  a. Antidifferentiation0
  b. Thing
  c. Undefined
  d. Undefined

18. _____ is a process of combining or accumulating. It may also refer to:
  a. Thing
  b. Integration0
  c. Undefined
  d. Undefined

19. In calculus, the indefinite integral of a given function i.e. the set of all antiderivatives of the function is always written with a constant, the _____.
  a. Thing
  b. Constant of integration0
  c. Undefined
  d. Undefined

20. _____ is a function that extends the concept of an ordinary sum

a. Integrand0
b. Thing
c. Undefined
d. Undefined

21. A _____ is a negotiable instrument instructing a financial institution to pay a specific amount of a specific currency from a specific demand account held in the maker/depositor's name with that institution. Both the maker and payee may be natural persons or legal entities.
    a. Check0
    b. Thing
    c. Undefined
    d. Undefined

22. _____ is the logarithm to the base e, where e is an irrational constant approximately equal to 2.718281828459.
    a. Natural logarithm0
    b. Thing
    c. Undefined
    d. Undefined

23. In mathematics, a _____ of a number x is the exponent y of the power by such that $x = b^y$. The value used for the base b must be neither 0 nor 1, nor a root of 1 in the case of the extension to complex numbers, and is typically 10, e, or 2.
    a. Logarithm0
    b. Thing
    c. Undefined
    d. Undefined

24. In mathematics, the _____ (or modulus) of a real number is its numerical value without regard to its sign.
    a. Absolute value0
    b. Thing
    c. Undefined
    d. Undefined

25. _____ is often used to describe the measurement of the steepness, incline, gradient, or grade of a straight line. The _____ is defined as the ratio of the "rise" divided by the "run" between two points on a line, or in other words, the ratio of the altitude change to the horizontal distance between any two points on the line.
    a. Thing
    b. Slope0
    c. Undefined
    d. Undefined

26. In mathematics, the concept of a _____ tries to capture the intuitive idea of a geometrical one-dimensional and continuous object. A simple example is the circle.
    a. Curve0
    b. Thing
    c. Undefined
    d. Undefined

27. In mathematics, _____ are the intuitive idea of a geometrical one-dimensional and continuous object.
    a. Curves0
    b. Thing
    c. Undefined
    d. Undefined

28. In mathematics, the _____ f is the collection of all ordered pairs . In particular, graph means the graphical representation of this collection, in the form of a curve or surface, together with axes, etc. Graphing on a Cartesian plane is sometimes referred to as curve sketching.
    a. Thing
    b. Graph of a function0
    c. Undefined
    d. Undefined

29. _____ are the basic objects of study in graph theory. Informally speaking, a graph is a set of objects called points, nodes, or vertices connected by links called lines or edges.

Chapter 6. Integration

a. Graphs0
b. Thing
c. Undefined
d. Undefined

30. A _____ is a special kind of ratio, indicating a relationship between two measurements with different units, such as miles to gallons or cents to pounds.
   a. Rate0
   b. Thing
   c. Undefined
   d. Undefined

31. In mathematics, an _____ is any of the arguments, i.e. "inputs", to a function. Thus if we have a function f(x), then x is a _____.
   a. Thing
   b. Independent variable0
   c. Undefined
   d. Undefined

32. In sociology and biology a _____ is the collection of people or organisms of a particular species living in a given geographic area or space, usually measured by a census.
   a. Thing
   b. Population0
   c. Undefined
   d. Undefined

33. _____ is change in population over time, and can be quantified as the change in the number of individuals in a population per unit time.
   a. Population growth0
   b. Thing
   c. Undefined
   d. Undefined

34. In a function the _____, is the variable which is the value, i.e. the "output", of the function.
   a. Dependent variable0
   b. Thing
   c. Undefined
   d. Undefined

35. The _____ of measurement are a globally standardized and modernized form of the metric system.
   a. Units0
   b. Thing
   c. Undefined
   d. Undefined

36. _____ is the change in total cost that arises when the quantity produced changes by one unit.
   a. Marginal cost0
   b. Thing
   c. Undefined
   d. Undefined

37. Fixed costs are expenses whose total does not change in proportion to the activity of a business.Unit fixed costs decline with volume following a retangular hyperbola as the volume of production.Variable costs by contrast change in relation to the activity of a business such as sales or production volume.Along with variable costs,fixed costs make up one of the two components of total cost. In the most simple production function total cost is equal to fixed costs plus variable costs.In accounting terminology, fixed costs will broadly include all costs which are not included in cost of goods sold, and variable costs are those captured in costs of goods sold. The implicit assumption required to make the equivalence between the accounting and economics terminology is that the accounting period is equal to the period in which fixed costs do not vary in relation to production. In practice, this equivalence does not always hold and depending on the period under consideration by management, some overhead expenses can be adjusted by management, and the specific allocation of each expense to each category will be decided under cost accounting.In business planning and management accounting, usage of the terms fixed costs, variable costs and others will often differ from usage in economics, and may depend on the intended use. For example, costs may be segregated into per unit costs fixed costs per period, and variable costs as a proportion of revenue. Capital expenditures will usually be allocated separately, and depending on the purpose, a portion may be regularly allocated to expenses as depreciation and amortization and seen as a _____ per period, or the entire amount may be considered upfront fixed costs.

   a. Thing
   b. Fixed cost0
   c. Undefined
   d. Undefined

38. _____ is the extra revenue that an additional unit of product will bring a firm. It can also be described as the change in total revenue/change in number of units sold.

   a. Marginal revenue0
   b. Thing
   c. Undefined
   d. Undefined

39. _____ is a business term for the amount of money that a company receives from its activities in a given period, mostly from sales of products and/or services to customers

   a. Revenue0
   b. Thing
   c. Undefined
   d. Undefined

40. _____ is a method for differentiating expressions involving exponentiation the power operation.

   a. Thing
   b. Power rule0
   c. Undefined
   d. Undefined

41. _____ is one of the most important functions in mathematics. A function commonly used to study growth and decay

   a. Thing
   b. Exponential function0
   c. Undefined
   d. Undefined

42. In mathematics, a _____ is the result of multiplying, or an expression that identifies factors to be multiplied.

   a. Thing
   b. Product0
   c. Undefined
   d. Undefined

43. A _____ is a set of numbers that designate location in a given reference system, such as x,y in a planar _____ system or an x,y,z in a three-dimensional _____ system.

   a. Coordinate0
   b. Thing
   c. Undefined
   d. Undefined

Chapter 6. Integration

44. In mathematics and its applications, a _____ is a system for assigning an n-tuple of numbers or scalars to each point in an n-dimensional space.
    a. Concept
    b. Coordinate system0
    c. Undefined
    d. Undefined

45. In common philosophical language, a proposition or _____, is the content of an assertion, that is, it is true-or-false and defined by the meaning of a particular piece of language.
    a. Statement0
    b. Concept
    c. Undefined
    d. Undefined

46. _____ are activities that are governed by a set of rules or customs and often engaged in competitively.
    a. Sports0
    b. Thing
    c. Undefined
    d. Undefined

47. In mathematics, an _____, mean, or central tendency of a data set refers to a measure of the "middle" or "expected" value of the data set.
    a. Average0
    b. Concept
    c. Undefined
    d. Undefined

48. _____ is the application of tools and a processing medium to the transformation of raw materials into finished goods for sale.
    a. Thing
    b. Manufacturing0
    c. Undefined
    d. Undefined

49. In the scientific method, an _____ (Latin: ex-+-periri, "of (or from) trying"), is a set of actions and observations, performed in the context of solving a particular problem or question, in order to support or falsify a hypothesis or research concerning phenomena.
    a. Thing
    b. Experiment0
    c. Undefined
    d. Undefined

50. A _____ function is a function for which, intuitively, small changes in the input result in small changes in the output.
    a. Continuous0
    b. Event
    c. Undefined
    d. Undefined

51. In calculus, the _____ is a formula for the derivative of the composite of two functions.
    a. Chain rule0
    b. Concept
    c. Undefined
    d. Undefined

52. _____ is a tool for finding antiderivatives and integrals. Using the fundamental theorem of calculus often requires finding an antiderivative. For this and other reasons, this rule is a relatively important tool for mathematicians. It is the counterpart to the chain rule of differentiation.
    a. Integration by substitution0
    b. Thing
    c. Undefined
    d. Undefined

53. A _____ is traditionally an infinitesimally small change in a variable.

a. Differential0
b. Thing
c. Undefined
d. Undefined

54. In mathematics, factorization (British English: factorisation) or factoring is the decomposition of an object (for example, a number, a polynomial, or a matrix) into a product of other objects, or _____, which when multiplied together give the original.
   a. Thing
   b. Factors0
   c. Undefined
   d. Undefined

55. The _____ is used to discard one of the variables in an equation, only to replace it with the actual value when solving multiple equations.
   a. Substitution method0
   b. Thing
   c. Undefined
   d. Undefined

56. In economics, supply and _____ describe market relations between prospective sellers and buyers of a good.
   a. Thing
   b. Demand0
   c. Undefined
   d. Undefined

57. _____, a field in mathematics, is the study of how functions change when their inputs change. The primary object of study in _____ is the derivative.
   a. Differential calculus0
   b. Thing
   c. Undefined
   d. Undefined

58. In mathematics, the conjugate _____ or adjoint matrix of an m-by-n matrix A with complex entries is the n-by-m matrix A* obtained from A by taking the transpose and then taking the complex conjugate of each entry.
   a. Pairs0
   b. Thing
   c. Undefined
   d. Undefined

59. _____ are expenses whose total does not change in proportion to the activity of a business, within the relevant time period or scale of production
   a. Thing
   b. Fixed costs0
   c. Undefined
   d. Undefined

60. Acid _____ ratio measures the ability of a company to use its near cash or quick assets to immediately extinguish its current liabilities.
   a. Thing
   b. Test0
   c. Undefined
   d. Undefined

61. _____ is a synonym for information.
   a. Thing
   b. Data0
   c. Undefined
   d. Undefined

62. In plane geometry, a _____ is a polygon with four equal sides, four right angles, and parallel opposite sides. In algebra, the _____ of a number is that number multiplied by itself.

a. Thing
b. Square0
c. Undefined
d. Undefined

63. Initial objects are also called _____, and terminal objects are also called final.
a. Thing
b. Coterminal0
c. Undefined
d. Undefined

64. In classical geometry, a _____ of a circle or sphere is any line segment from its center to its boundary. By extension, the _____ of a circle or sphere is the length of any such segment. The _____ is half the diameter. In science and engineering the term _____ of curvature is commonly used as a synonym for _____.
a. Radius0
b. Thing
c. Undefined
d. Undefined

65. _____ are a measure of time.
a. Minutes0
b. Thing
c. Undefined
d. Undefined

66. A _____ is a mathematical equation for an unknown function of one or several variables which relates the values of the function itself and of its derivatives of various orders.
a. Thing
b. Differential equation0
c. Undefined
d. Undefined

67. A _____ is a graphical tool to qualitatively visualize, or aid in numerical approximation of, solutions to differential equations.
a. Slope field0
b. Thing
c. Undefined
d. Undefined

68. In geometry, a line _____ is a part of a line that is bounded by two end points, and contains every point on the line between its end points.
a. Segment0
b. Concept
c. Undefined
d. Undefined

69. A _____ is a part of a line that is bounded by two end points, and contains every point on the line between its end points.
a. Thing
b. Line segment0
c. Undefined
d. Undefined

70. _____ is a kind of property which exists as magnitude or multitude. It is among the basic classes of things along with quality, substance, change, and relation.
a. Thing
b. Amount0
c. Undefined
d. Undefined

71. _____ is the fee paid on borrowed money.
a. Thing
b. Interest0
c. Undefined
d. Undefined

Chapter 6. Integration

72. _____ interest refers to the fact that whenever interest is calculated, it is based not only on the original principal, but also on any unpaid interest that has been added to the principal.
    a. Thing
    b. Compound0
    c. Undefined
    d. Undefined

73. _____ refers to the fact that whenever interest is calculated, it is based not only on the original principal, but also on any unpaid interest that has been added to the principal. The more frequently interest is compounded, the faster the balance grows.
    a. Concept
    b. Compound interest0
    c. Undefined
    d. Undefined

74. In mathematics, two quantities are called _____ if they vary in such a way that one of the quantities is a constant multiple of the other, or equivalently if they have a constant ratio.
    a. Thing
    b. Proportional0
    c. Undefined
    d. Undefined

75. In mathematics, _____ occurs when the growth rate of a function is always proportional to the function's current size.
    a. Exponential growth0
    b. Thing
    c. Undefined
    d. Undefined

76. _____ is the process in which an unstable atomic nucleus loses energy by emitting radiation in the form of particles or electromagnetic waves.
    a. Radioactive decay0
    b. Thing
    c. Undefined
    d. Undefined

77. The _____ is the total number of human beings alive on the planet Earth at a given time.
    a. Thing
    b. World population0
    c. Undefined
    d. Undefined

78. A _____ is 360° or 2∂ radians.
    a. Turn0
    b. Thing
    c. Undefined
    d. Undefined

79. A _____ is an abstract model that uses mathematical language to describe the behavior of a system. Eykhoff defined a _____ as 'a representation of the essential aspects of an existing system which presents knowledge of that system in usable form'.
    a. Mathematical model0
    b. Thing
    c. Undefined
    d. Undefined

80. _____ is a decrease that follows an exponential function.
    a. Exponential decay0
    b. Thing
    c. Undefined
    d. Undefined

81. A _____ models the S-curve of growth of some set P. The initial stage of growth is approximately exponential; then, as saturation begins, the growth slows, and at maturity, growth stops.

Chapter 6. Integration 79

a. Thing
b. Logistic function0
c. Undefined
d. Undefined

82. In epidemiology, an _____ is a disease that appears as new cases in a given human population, during a given period, at a rate that substantially exceeds with is "expected," based on recent experience.
a. Epidemic0
b. Thing
c. Undefined
d. Undefined

83. _____ is a special mathematical relationship between two quantities. Two quantities are called proportional if they vary in such a way that one of the quantities is a constant multiple of the other, or equivalently if they have a constant ratio.
a. Thing
b. Proportionality0
c. Undefined
d. Undefined

84. In mathematics and logic, a _____ proof is a way of showing the truth or falsehood of a given statement by a straightforward combination of established facts, usually existing lemmas and theorems, without making any further assumptions.
a. Direct0
b. Thing
c. Undefined
d. Undefined

85. _____ is electromagnetic radiation with a wavelength that is visible to the eye (visible _____) or, in a technical or scientific context, electromagnetic radiation of any wavelength.
a. Thing
b. Light0
c. Undefined
d. Undefined

86. In mathematics, a _____ is a two-dimensional manifold or surface that is perfectly flat.
a. Plane0
b. Thing
c. Undefined
d. Undefined

87. In geometry, a _____ is defined as a quadrilateral where all four of its angles are right angles.
a. Thing
b. Rectangle0
c. Undefined
d. Undefined

88. A _____ is the result of the addition of a set of numbers. The numbers may be natural numbers, complex numbers, matrices, or still more complicated objects. An infinite _____ is a subtle procedure known as a series.
a. Sum0
b. Thing
c. Undefined
d. Undefined

89. In mathematics, functions between ordered sets are _____ or monotone, or even isotone if they preserve the given order.
a. Thing
b. Monotonic0
c. Undefined
d. Undefined

90. An _____ is a straight line around which a geometric figure can be rotated.

a. Thing
b. Axis0
c. Undefined
d. Undefined

91. In mathematics, a _____ is the end result of a division problem. It can also be expressed as the number of times the divisor divides into the dividend.
a. Thing
b. Quotient0
c. Undefined
d. Undefined

92. An _____ is an increase, either of some fixed amount, for example added regularly, or of a variable amount.
a. Increment0
b. Thing
c. Undefined
d. Undefined

93. The function difference divided by the point difference is known as the _____
a. Thing
b. Difference quotient0
c. Undefined
d. Undefined

94. _____ is an adjective usually refering to being in the centre.
a. Central0
b. Thing
c. Undefined
d. Undefined

95. _____, Greek for "knowledge of nature," is the branch of science concerned with the discovery and characterization of universal laws which govern matter, energy, space, and time.
a. Physics0
b. Thing
c. Undefined
d. Undefined

96. _____, from Latin meaning "to make progress", is defined in two different ways. Pure economic _____ is the increase in wealth that an investor has from making an investment, taking into consideration all costs associated with that investment including the opportunity cost of capital.
a. Profit0
b. Thing
c. Undefined
d. Undefined

97. In topology and related areas of mathematics a _____ or Moore-Smith sequence is a generalization of a sequence, intended to unify the various notions of limit and generalize them to arbitrary topological spaces.
a. Thing
b. Net0
c. Undefined
d. Undefined

98. _____ is the transport of people on a trip/journey or the process or time involved in a person or object moving from one location to another.
a. Travel0
b. Thing
c. Undefined
d. Undefined

99. In mathematics, an inequality is a statement about the relative size or order of two objects. For example 14 > 10, or 14 is _____ 10.
a. Greater than0
b. Thing
c. Undefined
d. Undefined

Chapter 6. Integration

100. _____ is a function whose values do not vary and thus are constant.
 a. Thing
 b. Constant function0
 c. Undefined
 d. Undefined

101. _____ is the estimation of a physical quantity such as distance, energy, temperature, or time.
 a. Measurement0
 b. Thing
 c. Undefined
 d. Undefined

102. A _____ is a unit of length, usually used to measure distance, in a number of different systems, including Imperial units, United States customary units and Norwegian/Swedish mil. Its size can vary from system to system, but in each is between 1 and 10 kilometers. In contemporary English contexts _____ refers to either:
 a. Thing
 b. Mile0
 c. Undefined
 d. Undefined

103. _____ is a unit of speed, expressing the number of international miles covered per hour.
 a. Miles per hour0
 b. Thing
 c. Undefined
 d. Undefined

104. In mathematics, science including computer science, linguistics and engineering, an _____ is, generally speaking, an independent variable or input to a function.
 a. Thing
 b. Argument0
 c. Undefined
 d. Undefined

105. _____ are objects, characters, or other concrete representations of ideas, concepts, or other abstractions.
 a. Symbols0
 b. Thing
 c. Undefined
 d. Undefined

106. In mathematical logic, a Gödel numbering (or Gödel _____) is a function that assigns to each symbol and well-formed formula of some formal language a unique natural number called its Gödel number.
 a. Thing
 b. Code0
 c. Undefined
 d. Undefined

107. _____ is the middle point of a line segment.
 a. Midpoint0
 b. Thing
 c. Undefined
 d. Undefined

108. A _____ is a function for which, intuitively, small changes in the input result in small changes in the output.
 a. Event
 b. Continuous function0
 c. Undefined
 d. Undefined

109. _____ was a German mathematician who made important contributions to analysis and differential geometry, some of them paving the way for the later development of general relativity.
 a. Person
 b. Georg Riemann0
 c. Undefined
 d. Undefined

110. _____ is a method for approximating the values of integrals.

Chapter 6. Integration

    a. Riemann sum0
    b. Thing
    c. Undefined
    d. Undefined

111. _____ is a mathematical subject that includes the study of limits, derivatives, integrals, and power series and constitutes a major part of modern university curriculum.
    a. Thing
    b. Calculus0
    c. Undefined
    d. Undefined

112. In number theory, the _____ of arithmetic (or unique factorization theorem) states that every natural number greater than 1 can be written as a unique product of prime numbers.
    a. Fundamental theorem0
    b. Concept
    c. Undefined
    d. Undefined

113. _____ of calculus is the statement that the two central operations of calculus, differentiation and integration, are inverse operations: if a continuous function is first integrated and then differentiated, the original function is retrieved.
    a. Thing
    b. Fundamental Theorem of Calculus0
    c. Undefined
    d. Undefined

114. In mathematics, especially in order theory, an _____ of a subset S of some partially ordered set is an element of P which is greater than or equal to every element of S.
    a. Thing
    b. Upper bound0
    c. Undefined
    d. Undefined

115. _____ is a physical property of a system that underlies the common notions of hot and cold; something that is hotter has the greater _____.
    a. Temperature0
    b. Thing
    c. Undefined
    d. Undefined

116. A _____ is a deliberate process for transforming one or more inputs into one or more results.
    a. Thing
    b. Calculation0
    c. Undefined
    d. Undefined

117. _____ constitutes a broad family of algorithms for calculating the numerical value of a definite integral, and by extension, the term is also sometimes used to describe the numerical solution of differential equations.
    a. Numerical integration0
    b. Thing
    c. Undefined
    d. Undefined

118. In business, particularly accounting, a _____ is the time intervals that the accounts, statement, payments, or other calculations cover.
    a. Period0
    b. Thing
    c. Undefined
    d. Undefined

119. _____ is a list of goods and materials, or those goods and materials themselves, held available in stock by a business

Chapter 6. Integration

    a. Thing
    c. Undefined
    b. Inventory0
    d. Undefined

120. The _____ of a solid object is the three-dimensional concept of how much space it occupies, often quantified numerically.
    a. Volume0
    c. Undefined
    b. Thing
    d. Undefined

121. An _____ of a product of sums expresses it as a sum of products by using the fact that multiplication distributes over addition.
    a. Expansion0
    c. Undefined
    b. Thing
    d. Undefined

122. _____ of a population is the number of childbirths per 1,000 persons per year
    a. Birth rate0
    c. Undefined
    b. Thing
    d. Undefined

123. A _____ is a vehicle, missile or aircraft which obtains thrust by the reaction to the ejection of fast moving fluid from within a _____ engine.
    a. Rocket0
    c. Undefined
    b. Thing
    d. Undefined

124. The word _____ comes from the Latin word linearis, which means created by lines.
    a. Linear0
    c. Undefined
    b. Thing
    d. Undefined

125. U.S. liquid _____ is legally defined as 231 cubic inches, and is equal to 3.785411784 litres or abotu 0.13368 cubic feet. This is the most common definition of a _____. The U.S. fluid ounce is defined as 1/128 of a U.S. _____.
    a. Thing
    c. Undefined
    b. Gallon0
    d. Undefined

126. A _____ is a quadrilateral, which is defined as a shape with four sides, which has a pair of parallel sides.
    a. Thing
    c. Undefined
    b. Trapezoid0
    d. Undefined

127. The _____ function (weight function) is a mathematical device used when performing a sum, integral, or average in order to give some elements more of a "weight" than others.
    a. Weighted0
    c. Undefined
    b. Thing
    d. Undefined

128. A _____ is often used in statistics.
    a. Thing
    c. Undefined
    b. Weighted mean0
    d. Undefined

Chapter 6. Integration

129. In trigonometry, the _____ is a function defined as tan x = $^{\sin x}/_{\cos x}$. The function is so-named because it can be defined as the length of a certain segment of a _____ (in the geometric sense) to the unit circle. In plane geometry, a line is _____ to a curve, at some point, if both line and curve pass through the point with the same direction.
 a. Tangent0
 b. Thing
 c. Undefined
 d. Undefined

130. _____ has two distinct but etymologically-related meanings: one in geometry and one in trigonometry.
 a. Thing
 b. Tangent line0
 c. Undefined
 d. Undefined

131. _____ the American term is a way to approximately calculate the definite integral
 a. Thing
 b. Trapezoidal Rule0
 c. Undefined
 d. Undefined

132. In mathematics, there are several meanings of _____ depending on the subject.
 a. Thing
 b. Degree0
 c. Undefined
 d. Undefined

133. In mathematics, a _____ is an expression that is constructed from one or more variables and constants, using only the operations of addition, subtraction, multiplication, and constant positive whole number exponents. is a _____. Note in particular that division by an expression containing a variable is not in general allowed in polynomials. [1]
 a. Thing
 b. Polynomial0
 c. Undefined
 d. Undefined

134. In mathematics, computing, linguistics, and related disciplines, an _____ is a finite list of well-defined instructions for accomplishing some task which, given an initial state, will terminate in a defined end-state.
 a. Algorithm0
 b. Concept
 c. Undefined
 d. Undefined

135. According to the United Nations Statistics Division, _____ is the resale sale without transformation of new and used goods to retailers, to industrial, commercial, institutional or professional users, or to other wholesalers, or involves acting as an agent or broker in buying merchandise for, or selling merchandise, to such persons or companies.
 a. Thing
 b. Wholesale0
 c. Undefined
 d. Undefined

136. _____ is the chance that something is likely to happen or be the case.
 a. Thing
 b. Probability0
 c. Undefined
 d. Undefined

137. _____ is a function that represents a probability distribution in terms of integrals.
 a. Probability density function0
 b. Thing
 c. Undefined
 d. Undefined

138. _____ of a probability distribution, random variable, or population or multiset of values is a measure of the spread of its values.

Chapter 6. Integration 85

a. Standard deviation0
b. Thing
c. Undefined
d. Undefined

139. The _____, the average in everyday English, which is also called the arithmetic _____ (and is distinguished from the geometric _____ or harmonic _____). The average is also called the sample _____. The expected value of a random variable, which is also called the population _____.
 a. Thing
 b. Mean0
 c. Undefined
 d. Undefined

140. A _____ is a function that assigns a number to subsets of a given set.
 a. Thing
 b. Measure0
 c. Undefined
 d. Undefined

141. _____ is a subset of a population.
 a. Sample0
 b. Thing
 c. Undefined
 d. Undefined

142. _____ is mass m per unit volume V.
 a. Thing
 b. Density0
 c. Undefined
 d. Undefined

143. _____ is a measure of difference for interval and ratio variables between the observed value and the mean.
 a. Deviation0
 b. Thing
 c. Undefined
 d. Undefined

144. In mathematics, a statistical _____ of a set of data is a measure how observations in the data set are distributed across various categories.
 a. Thing
 b. Dispersion0
 c. Undefined
 d. Undefined

Chapter 7. Additional Integration Topics

1. A _____ is the result of the addition of a set of numbers. The numbers may be natural numbers, complex numbers, matrices, or still more complicated objects. An infinite _____ is a subtle procedure known as a series.
   a. Sum0
   b. Thing
   c. Undefined
   d. Undefined

2. In mathematics, the concept of a _____ tries to capture the intuitive idea of a geometrical one-dimensional and continuous object. A simple example is the circle.
   a. Thing
   b. Curve0
   c. Undefined
   d. Undefined

3. In mathematics, _____ are the intuitive idea of a geometrical one-dimensional and continuous object.
   a. Curves0
   b. Thing
   c. Undefined
   d. Undefined

4. _____ is an extension of the concept of a sum.
   a. Thing
   b. Definite integral0
   c. Undefined
   d. Undefined

5. An _____ is a straight line around which a geometric figure can be rotated.
   a. Thing
   b. Axis0
   c. Undefined
   d. Undefined

6. The _____ of a function is an extension of the concept of a sum, and are identified or found through the use of integration.
   a. Thing
   b. Integral0
   c. Undefined
   d. Undefined

7. In mathematical analysis, _____ are objects which generalize functions and probability distributions.
   a. Thing
   b. Distribution0
   c. Undefined
   d. Undefined

8. The mathematical concept of a _____ expresses the intuitive idea of deterministic dependence between two quantities, one of which is viewed as primary and the other as secondary. A _____ then is a way to associate a unique output for each input of a specified type, for example, a real number or an element of a given set.
   a. Thing
   b. Function0
   c. Undefined
   d. Undefined

9. In elementary algebra, an _____ is a set that contains every real number between two indicated numbers and may contain the two numbers themselves.
   a. Thing
   b. Interval0
   c. Undefined
   d. Undefined

10. In mathematics, the _____ f is the collection of all ordered pairs . In particular, graph means the graphical representation of this collection, in the form of a curve or surface, together with axes, etc. Graphing on a Cartesian plane is sometimes referred to as curve sketching.

a. Graph of a function0 b. Thing
c. Undefined d. Undefined

11. A _____ is a set of numbers that designate location in a given reference system, such as x,y in a planar _____ system or an x,y,z in a three-dimensional _____ system.
   a. Thing b. Coordinate0
   c. Undefined d. Undefined

12. In mathematics and its applications, a _____ is a system for assigning an n-tuple of numbers or scalars to each point in an n-dimensional space.
   a. Concept b. Coordinate system0
   c. Undefined d. Undefined

13. In mathematics, a _____ is the result of multiplying, or an expression that identifies factors to be multiplied.
   a. Thing b. Product0
   c. Undefined d. Undefined

14. In geometry, a _____ is defined as a quadrilateral where all four of its angles are right angles.
   a. Rectangle0 b. Thing
   c. Undefined d. Undefined

15. In mathematical analysis and related areas of mathematics, a set is called _____, if it is, in a certain sense, of finite size.
   a. Thing b. Bounded0
   c. Undefined d. Undefined

16. A _____ function is a function for which, intuitively, small changes in the input result in small changes in the output.
   a. Event b. Continuous0
   c. Undefined d. Undefined

17. _____ are the basic objects of study in graph theory. Informally speaking, a graph is a set of objects called points, nodes, or vertices connected by links called lines or edges.
   a. Thing b. Graphs0
   c. Undefined d. Undefined

18. _____ is a method for approximating the values of integrals.
   a. Riemann sum0 b. Thing
   c. Undefined d. Undefined

19. In mathematics, the _____ of two sets A and B is the set that contains all elements of A that also belong to B (or equivalently, all elements of B that also belong to A), but no other elements.
   a. Thing b. Intersection0
   c. Undefined d. Undefined

20. A _____ is a negotiable instrument instructing a financial institution to pay a specific amount of a specific currency from a specific demand account held in the maker/depositor's name with that institution. Both the maker and payee may be natural persons or legal entities.
- a. Thing
- b. Check0
- c. Undefined
- d. Undefined

21. _____ constitutes a broad family of algorithms for calculating the numerical value of a definite integral, and by extension, the term is also sometimes used to describe the numerical solution of differential equations.
- a. Numerical integration0
- b. Thing
- c. Undefined
- d. Undefined

22. _____ is a process of combining or accumulating. It may also refer to:
- a. Integration0
- b. Thing
- c. Undefined
- d. Undefined

23. In mathematics, the _____ is a conic section generated by the intersection of a right circular conical surface and a plane parallel to a generating straight line of that surface. It can also be defined as locus of points in a plane which are equidistant from a given point.
- a. Parabola0
- b. Thing
- c. Undefined
- d. Undefined

24. _____ is a synonym for information.
- a. Thing
- b. Data0
- c. Undefined
- d. Undefined

25. In mathematics, an _____ is a statement about the relative size or order of two objects.
- a. Thing
- b. Inequality0
- c. Undefined
- d. Undefined

26. _____ is a way of expressing a number as a fraction of 100 per cent meaning "per hundred".
- a. Percent0
- b. Thing
- c. Undefined
- d. Undefined

27. A _____ is a symbolic representation denoting a quantity or expression. It often represents an "unknown" quantity that has the potential to change.
- a. Thing
- b. Variable0
- c. Undefined
- d. Undefined

28. Two mathematical objects are equal if and only if they are precisely the same in every way. This defines a binary relation, _____, denoted by the sign of _____ "=" in such a way that the statement "x = y" means that x and y are equal.
- a. Equality0
- b. Thing
- c. Undefined
- d. Undefined

29. A _____ is one of the basic shapes of geometry: a polygon with three vertices and three sides which are straight line segments.

a. Triangle0
b. Thing
c. Undefined
d. Undefined

30. A _____ is a quantity that denotes the proportional amount or magnitude of one quantity relative to another.
    a. Thing
    b. Ratio0
    c. Undefined
    d. Undefined

31. The word _____ is used in a variety of ways in mathematics.
    a. Index0
    b. Thing
    c. Undefined
    d. Undefined

32. A _____ is a function that assigns a number to subsets of a given set.
    a. Thing
    b. Measure0
    c. Undefined
    d. Undefined

33. A _____ is a special kind of ratio, indicating a relationship between two measurements with different units, such as miles to gallons or cents to pounds.
    a. Rate0
    b. Thing
    c. Undefined
    d. Undefined

34. _____ are economic entities that give rise to future economic benefit and is controlled by the entity as a result of past transaction or other events
    a. Asset0
    b. Thing
    c. Undefined
    d. Undefined

35. In economics, supply and _____ describe market relations between prospective sellers and buyers of a good.
    a. Demand0
    b. Thing
    c. Undefined
    d. Undefined

36. In the scientific method, an _____ (Latin: ex-+-periri, "of (or from) trying"), is a set of actions and observations, performed in the context of solving a particular problem or question, in order to support or falsify a hypothesis or research concerning phenomena.
    a. Thing
    b. Experiment0
    c. Undefined
    d. Undefined

37. In mathematics, two quantities are called _____ if they vary in such a way that one of the quantities is a constant multiple of the other, or equivalently if they have a constant ratio.
    a. Thing
    b. Proportional0
    c. Undefined
    d. Undefined

38. In mathematics, an _____, mean, or central tendency of a data set refers to a measure of the "middle" or "expected" value of the data set.
    a. Concept
    b. Average0
    c. Undefined
    d. Undefined

39. _____ is the chance that something is likely to happen or be the case.

Chapter 7. Additional Integration Topics

    a. Probability0
    b. Thing
    c. Undefined
    d. Undefined

40. _____ is a function that represents a probability distribution in terms of integrals.
    a. Thing
    b. Probability density function0
    c. Undefined
    d. Undefined

41. A _____ is an individual or household that purchases and uses goods and services generated within the economy.
    a. Thing
    b. Consumer0
    c. Undefined
    d. Undefined

42. _____ is a regular and continuing flow of money generated by a business or investment
    a. Income stream0
    b. Thing
    c. Undefined
    d. Undefined

43. _____ is mass m per unit volume V.
    a. Density0
    b. Thing
    c. Undefined
    d. Undefined

44. An _____ is the limit of a definite integral, as an endpoint of the interval of integration approaches either a specified real number or ‡ or − ‡ or, in some cases, as both endpoints approach limits.
    a. Improper integral0
    b. Thing
    c. Undefined
    d. Undefined

45. _____ is a quantity whose values are random and to which a probability distribution is assigned.
    a. Random variable0
    b. Thing
    c. Undefined
    d. Undefined

46. In mathematics, an _____ is any of the arguments, i.e. "inputs", to a function. Thus if we have a function f(x), then x is a _____.
    a. Independent variable0
    b. Thing
    c. Undefined
    d. Undefined

47. _____ are a measure of time.
    a. Minutes0
    b. Thing
    c. Undefined
    d. Undefined

48. A _____ is a function for which, intuitively, small changes in the input result in small changes in the output.
    a. Event
    b. Continuous function0
    c. Undefined
    d. Undefined

49. In statistics, a _____ measure is one which is measuring what is supposed to measure.
    a. Thing
    b. Valid0
    c. Undefined
    d. Undefined

Chapter 7. Additional Integration Topics

50. In mathematics and the mathematical sciences, a _____ is a fixed, but possibly unspecified, value. This is in contrast to a variable, which is not fixed.
    a. Constant0
    b. Thing
    c. Undefined
    d. Undefined

51. _____ measures the nominal future sum of money that a given sum of money is "worth" at a specified time in the future assuming a certain interest rate; this value does not include corrections for inflation or other factors that affect the true value of money in the future.
    a. Future value0
    b. Thing
    c. Undefined
    d. Undefined

52. _____ is the fee paid on borrowed money.
    a. Interest0
    b. Thing
    c. Undefined
    d. Undefined

53. In business, particularly accounting, a _____ is the time intervals that the accounts, statement, payments, or other calculations cover.
    a. Period0
    b. Thing
    c. Undefined
    d. Undefined

54. An _____ is the fee paid on borrow money.
    a. Concept
    b. Interest rate0
    c. Undefined
    d. Undefined

55. In economics, economic _____ is simply a state of the world where economic forces are balanced and in the absence of external influences the values of economic variables will not change.
    a. Thing
    b. Equilibrium0
    c. Undefined
    d. Undefined

56. _____ is the price at which the quantity demanded of a good or service is equal to the quantity supplied.
    a. Thing
    b. Equilibrium price0
    c. Undefined
    d. Undefined

57. An _____ is a combination of numbers, operators, grouping symbols and/or free variables and bound variables arranged in a meaningful way which can be evaluated..
    a. Expression0
    b. Thing
    c. Undefined
    d. Undefined

58. _____ is a statistical measure of the average length of survival of a living thing.
    a. Thing
    b. Life expectancy0
    c. Undefined
    d. Undefined

59. The Yakovlev Yak-25, NATO designation _____-A / Mandrake, was a swept wing, turbojet-powered interceptor aircraft and reconnaissance aircraft used by the Soviet Union.

a. Flashlight0
b. Thing
c. Undefined
d. Undefined

60. _____ or investing is a term with several closely-related meanings in business management, finance and economics, related to saving or deferring consumption.
   a. Thing
   b. Investment0
   c. Undefined
   d. Undefined

61. Initial objects are also called _____, and terminal objects are also called final.
   a. Coterminal0
   b. Thing
   c. Undefined
   d. Undefined

62. _____ of a single or multiple future payments is the nominal amounts of money to change hands at some future date, discounted to account for the time value of money, and other factors such as investment risk.
   a. Thing
   b. Present value0
   c. Undefined
   d. Undefined

63. The word _____ comes from the Latin word linearis, which means created by lines.
   a. Thing
   b. Linear0
   c. Undefined
   d. Undefined

64. _____ is a regression method that models the relationship between a dependent variable Y, independent variables X_p, and a random term å.
   a. Thing
   b. Linear regression0
   c. Undefined
   d. Undefined

65. An _____ of a function f is a function F whose derivative is equal to f, i.e., F' = f.
   a. Antiderivative0
   b. Thing
   c. Undefined
   d. Undefined

66. The _____ is a measurement of how a function changes when the values of its inputs change.
   a. Derivative0
   b. Thing
   c. Undefined
   d. Undefined

67. In calculus, the indefinite integral of a given function i.e. the set of all antiderivatives of the function is always written with a constant, the _____.
   a. Constant of integration0
   b. Thing
   c. Undefined
   d. Undefined

68. The _____, the average in everyday English, which is also called the arithmetic _____ (and is distinguished from the geometric _____ or harmonic _____). The average is also called the sample _____. The expected value of a random variable, which is also called the population _____.
   a. Mean0
   b. Thing
   c. Undefined
   d. Undefined

69. _____ is a function that extends the concept of an ordinary sum

Chapter 7. Additional Integration Topics

a. Integrand0
c. Undefined
b. Thing
d. Undefined

70. _____ is the logarithm to the base e, where e is an irrational constant approximately equal to 2.718281828459.
    a. Natural logarithm0
    c. Undefined
    b. Thing
    d. Undefined

71. In mathematics, a _____ of a number x is the exponent y of the power by such that $x = b^y$. The value used for the base b must be neither 0 nor 1, nor a root of 1 in the case of the extension to complex numbers, and is typically 10, e, or 2.
    a. Logarithm0
    c. Undefined
    b. Thing
    d. Undefined

72. _____, from Latin meaning "to make progress", is defined in two different ways. Pure economic _____ is the increase in wealth that an investor has from making an investment, taking into consideration all costs associated with that investment including the opportunity cost of capital.
    a. Profit0
    c. Undefined
    b. Thing
    d. Undefined

73. _____ is the application of tools and a processing medium to the transformation of raw materials into finished goods for sale.
    a. Manufacturing0
    c. Undefined
    b. Thing
    d. Undefined

74. _____ is a kind of property which exists as magnitude or multitude. It is among the basic classes of things along with quality, substance, change, and relation.
    a. Amount0
    c. Undefined
    b. Thing
    d. Undefined

75. In mathematics, _____ refers to the rewriting of an expression into a simpler form.
    a. Thing
    c. Undefined
    b. Reduction0
    d. Undefined

76. In mathematics, the conjugate _____ or adjoint matrix of an m-by-n matrix A with complex entries is the n-by-m matrix A* obtained from A by taking the transpose and then taking the complex conjugate of each entry.
    a. Thing
    c. Undefined
    b. Pairs0
    d. Undefined

77. _____ is the change in total cost that arises when the quantity produced changes by one unit.
    a. Marginal cost0
    c. Undefined
    b. Thing
    d. Undefined

Chapter 7. Additional Integration Topics

78. Fixed costs are expenses whose total does not change in proportion to the activity of a business. Unit fixed costs decline with volume following a retangular hyperbola as the volume of production. Variable costs by contrast change in relation to the activity of a business such as sales or production volume. Along with variable costs, fixed costs make up one of the two components of total cost. In the most simple production function total cost is equal to fixed costs plus variable costs. In accounting terminology, fixed costs will broadly include all costs which are not included in cost of goods sold, and variable costs are those captured in costs of goods sold. The implicit assumption required to make the equivalence between the accounting and economics terminology is that the accounting period is equal to the period in which fixed costs do not vary in relation to production. In practice, this equivalence does not always hold and depending on the period under consideration by management, some overhead expenses can be adjusted by management, and the specific allocation of each expense to each category will be decided under cost accounting. In business planning and management accounting, usage of the terms fixed costs, variable costs and others will often differ from usage in economics, and may depend on the intended use. For example, costs may be segregated into per unit costs fixed costs per period, and variable costs as a proportion of revenue. Capital expenditures will usually be allocated separately, and depending on the purpose, a portion may be regularly allocated to expenses as depreciation and amortization and seen as a _____ per period, or the entire amount may be considered upfront fixed costs.
    a. Fixed cost0
    b. Thing
    c. Undefined
    d. Undefined

79. _____ are expenses whose total does not change in proportion to the activity of a business, within the relevant time period or scale of production
    a. Fixed costs0
    b. Thing
    c. Undefined
    d. Undefined

80. Acid _____ ratio measures the ability of a company to use its near cash or quick assets to immediately extinguish its current liabilities.
    a. Test0
    b. Thing
    c. Undefined
    d. Undefined

81. In finance and economics, _____ is the process of finding the present value of an amount of cash at some future date, and along with compounding cash forms the basis of time value of money calculations.
    a. Thing
    b. Discount0
    c. Undefined
    d. Undefined

82. _____ is the extra revenue that an additional unit of product will bring a firm. It can also be described as the change in total revenue/change in number of units sold.
    a. Marginal revenue0
    b. Thing
    c. Undefined
    d. Undefined

83. _____ is a business term for the amount of money that a company receives from its activities in a given period, mostly from sales of products and/or services to customers
    a. Revenue0
    b. Thing
    c. Undefined
    d. Undefined

84. In classical geometry, a _____ of a circle or sphere is any line segment from its center to its boundary. By extension, the _____ of a circle or sphere is the length of any such segment. The _____ is half the diameter. In science and engineering the term _____ of curvature is commonly used as a synonym for _____.

a. Radius0
b. Thing
c. Undefined
d. Undefined

85. _____ are objects, characters, or other concrete representations of ideas, concepts, or other abstractions.
   a. Symbols0
   b. Thing
   c. Undefined
   d. Undefined

86. An _____ is when two lines intersect somewhere on a plane creating a right angle at intersection
   a. Thing
   b. Axes0
   c. Undefined
   d. Undefined

87. In sociology and biology a _____ is the collection of people or organisms of a particular species living in a given geographic area or space, usually measured by a census.
   a. Thing
   b. Population0
   c. Undefined
   d. Undefined

88. In plane geometry, a _____ is a polygon with four equal sides, four right angles, and parallel opposite sides. In algebra, the _____ of a number is that number multiplied by itself.
   a. Thing
   b. Square0
   c. Undefined
   d. Undefined

89. _____ is a concept that permeates much of inferential statistics and descriptive statistics. More properly, it is "the sum of the squared deviations".
   a. Sum of squares0
   b. Thing
   c. Undefined
   d. Undefined

90. In economics, _____ describe market relations between prospective sellers and buyers of a good.
   a. Supply and demand0
   b. Thing
   c. Undefined
   d. Undefined

91. In mathematics, a _____ set is the complement of a meager set. A meager set is one which is the countable union of nowhere dense sets.
   a. Thing
   b. Residual0
   c. Undefined
   d. Undefined

Chapter 8. Multivariable Calculus

1. A _____ is a symbolic representation denoting a quantity or expression. It often represents an "unknown" quantity that has the potential to change.
   a. Variable0
   b. Thing
   c. Undefined
   d. Undefined

2. In mathematics, an _____ is any of the arguments, i.e. "inputs", to a function. Thus if we have a function f(x), then x is a _____.
   a. Thing
   b. Independent variable0
   c. Undefined
   d. Undefined

3. The mathematical concept of a _____ expresses the intuitive idea of deterministic dependence between two quantities, one of which is viewed as primary and the other as secondary. A _____ then is a way to associate a unique output for each input of a specified type, for example, a real number or an element of a given set.
   a. Function0
   b. Thing
   c. Undefined
   d. Undefined

4. In mathematics, a _____ is the result of multiplying, or an expression that identifies factors to be multiplied.
   a. Product0
   b. Thing
   c. Undefined
   d. Undefined

5. _____ is the application of tools and a processing medium to the transformation of raw materials into finished goods for sale.
   a. Manufacturing0
   b. Thing
   c. Undefined
   d. Undefined

6. Fixed costs are expenses whose total does not change in proportion to the activity of a business.Unit fixed costs decline with volume following a retangular hyperbola as the volume of production.Variable costs by contrast change in relation to the activity of a business such as sales or production volume.Along with variable costs,fixed costs make up one of the two components of total cost. In the most simple production function total cost is equal to fixed costs plus variable costs.In accounting terminology, fixed costs will broadly include all costs which are not included in cost of goods sold, and variable costs are those captured in costs of goods sold. The implicit assumption required to make the equivalence between the accounting and economics terminology is that the accounting period is equal to the period in which fixed costs do not vary in relation to production. In practice, this equivalence does not always hold and depending on the period under consideration by management, some overhead expenses can be adjusted by management, and the specific allocation of each expense to each category will be decided under cost accounting.In business planning and management accounting, usage of the terms fixed costs, variable costs and others will often differ from usage in economics, and may depend on the intended use. For example, costs may be segregated into per unit costs fixed costs per period, and variable costs as a proportion of revenue. Capital expenditures will usually be allocated separately, and depending on the purpose, a portion may be regularly allocated to expenses as depreciation and amortization and seen as a _____ per period, or the entire amount may be considered upfront fixed costs.
   a. Thing
   b. Fixed cost0
   c. Undefined
   d. Undefined

7. _____ are expenses whose total does not change in proportion to the activity of a business, within the relevant time period or scale of production

a. Thing
b. Fixed costs0
c. Undefined
d. Undefined

8. An _____ is a collection of two not necessarily distinct objects, one of which is distinguished as the first coordinate and the other as the second coordinate.
a. Thing
b. Ordered pair0
c. Undefined
d. Undefined

9. In a function the _____, is the variable which is the value, i.e. the "output", of the function.
a. Dependent variable0
b. Thing
c. Undefined
d. Undefined

10. In mathematics, the _____ of a function is the set of all "output" values produced by that function. Given a function $f : A \to B$, the _____ of f, is defined to be the set $\{x \in B : x = f(a) \text{ for some } a \in A\}$.
a. Range0
b. Thing
c. Undefined
d. Undefined

11. In mathematics, the conjugate _____ or adjoint matrix of an m-by-n matrix A with complex entries is the n-by-m matrix A* obtained from A by taking the transpose and then taking the complex conjugate of each entry.
a. Thing
b. Pairs0
c. Undefined
d. Undefined

12. In mathematics, a _____ of a k-place relation $L \subseteq X_1 \times \ldots \times X_k$ is one of the sets X_j, $1 \leq j \leq k$. In the special case where k = 2 and $L \subseteq X_1 \times X_2$ is a function $L : X_1 \to X_2$, it is conventional to refer to X_1 as the _____ of the function and to refer to X_2 as the codomain of the function.
a. Domain0
b. Thing
c. Undefined
d. Undefined

13. In mathematics, a _____ may be described informally as a number that can be given by an infinite decimal representation.
a. Thing
b. Real number0
c. Undefined
d. Undefined

14. The _____ of measurement are a globally standardized and modernized form of the metric system.
a. Units0
b. Thing
c. Undefined
d. Undefined

15. A _____ is a set of numbers that designate location in a given reference system, such as x,y in a planar _____ system or an x,y,z in a three-dimensional _____ system.
a. Thing
b. Coordinate0
c. Undefined
d. Undefined

16. In mathematics and its applications, a _____ is a system for assigning an n-tuple of numbers or scalars to each point in an n-dimensional space.

a. Concept
c. Undefined
b. Coordinate system0
d. Undefined

17. In mathematics and its applications, _____ are used for assigning an n-tuple of numbers or scalars to each point in an n-dimensional space.
   a. Concept
   b. Coordinate systems0
   c. Undefined
   d. Undefined

18. _____ are the basic objects of study in graph theory. Informally speaking, a graph is a set of objects called points, nodes, or vertices connected by links called lines or edges.
   a. Thing
   b. Graphs0
   c. Undefined
   d. Undefined

19. A _____ is a one-dimensional picture in which the integers are shown as specially-marked points evenly spaced on a line.
   a. Number line0
   b. Thing
   c. Undefined
   d. Undefined

20. In mathematics, the _____ of a coordinate system is the point where the axes of the system intersect.
   a. Thing
   b. Origin0
   c. Undefined
   d. Undefined

21. In geometry, two lines or planes if one falls on the other in such a way as to create congruent adjacent angles. The term may be used as a noun or adjective. Thus, referring to Figure 1, the line AB is the _____ to CD through the point B.
   a. Perpendicular0
   b. Thing
   c. Undefined
   d. Undefined

22. In geometry, _____ lines are two lines that share one or more common points.
   a. Intersecting0
   b. Thing
   c. Undefined
   d. Undefined

23. In mathematics, the _____ is a conic section generated by the intersection of a right circular conical surface and a plane parallel to a generating straight line of that surface. It can also be defined as locus of points in a plane which are equidistant from a given point.
   a. Parabola0
   b. Thing
   c. Undefined
   d. Undefined

24. In mathematics, a _____ is a two-dimensional manifold or surface that is perfectly flat.
   a. Plane0
   b. Thing
   c. Undefined
   d. Undefined

25. An _____ is a straight line around which a geometric figure can be rotated.
   a. Thing
   b. Axis0
   c. Undefined
   d. Undefined

26. _____ is a quadric

a. Paraboloid0   b. Thing
c. Undefined   d. Undefined

27. A real-valued function f defined on the real line is said to have a _____ point at the point x∗, if there exists some ε > 0, such that f when x − x∗ < ε.
   a. Thing   b. Local maximum0
   c. Undefined   d. Undefined

28. In the most general terms, a _____ for a smooth function (curve, surface or hypersurface) is a point such that the curve/surface/etc. in the neighborhood of this point lies on different sides of the tangent at this point. In certain contexts the definition may vary. It is most frequently used at critical points.
   a. Thing   b. Saddle point0
   c. Undefined   d. Undefined

29. In mathematics, the _____ f is the collection of all ordered pairs . In particular, graph means the graphical representation of this collection, in the form of a curve or surface, together with axes, etc. Graphing on a Cartesian plane is sometimes referred to as curve sketching.
   a. Thing   b. Graph of a function0
   c. Undefined   d. Undefined

30. In mathematics, _____ are two-dimensional manifolds or surfaces that are perfectly flat.
   a. Planes0   b. Thing
   c. Undefined   d. Undefined

31. _____ are external two-dimensional outlines, with the appearance or configuration of some thing - in contrast to the matter or content or substance of which it is composed.
   a. Thing   b. Shapes0
   c. Undefined   d. Undefined

32. In geometry, the _____ of an object is a point in some sense in the middle of the object.
   a. Center0   b. Thing
   c. Undefined   d. Undefined

33. In Euclidean geometry, a _____ is the set of all points in a plane at a fixed distance, called the radius, from a given point, the center.
   a. Thing   b. Circle0
   c. Undefined   d. Undefined

34. _____ is a business term for the amount of money that a company receives from its activities in a given period, mostly from sales of products and/or services to customers
   a. Revenue0   b. Thing
   c. Undefined   d. Undefined

35. _____, from Latin meaning "to make progress", is defined in two different ways. Pure economic _____ is the increase in wealth that an investor has from making an investment, taking into consideration all costs associated with that investment including the opportunity cost of capital.

a. Thing
b. Profit0
c. Undefined
d. Undefined

36. In economics, supply and _____ describe market relations between prospective sellers and buyers of a good.
a. Thing
b. Demand0
c. Undefined
d. Undefined

37. _____ asserts that the maximum output of a technologically-determined production process is a mathematical function of input factors of production.
a. Production function0
b. Thing
c. Undefined
d. Undefined

38. _____ is a kind of property which exists as magnitude or multitude. It is among the basic classes of things along with quality, substance, change, and relation.
a. Thing
b. Amount0
c. Undefined
d. Undefined

39. A _____ is a special kind of ratio, indicating a relationship between two measurements with different units, such as miles to gallons or cents to pounds.
a. Rate0
b. Thing
c. Undefined
d. Undefined

40. In business, particularly accounting, a _____ is the time intervals that the accounts, statement, payments, or other calculations cover.
a. Thing
b. Period0
c. Undefined
d. Undefined

41. _____ is the income from capital investment paid in a series of regular payments.
a. Annuity0
b. Thing
c. Undefined
d. Undefined

42. _____ is the fee paid on borrowed money.
a. Thing
b. Interest0
c. Undefined
d. Undefined

43. _____ measures the nominal future sum of money that a given sum of money is "worth" at a specified time in the future assuming a certain interest rate; this value does not include corrections for inflation or other factors that affect the true value of money in the future.
a. Future value0
b. Thing
c. Undefined
d. Undefined

44. The _____ of a solid object is the three-dimensional concept of how much space it occupies, often quantified numerically.
a. Thing
b. Volume0
c. Undefined
d. Undefined

Chapter 8. Multivariable Calculus

45. _____ is the flow of blood in the cardiovascular system.
    a. Thing
    b. Blood flow0
    c. Undefined
    d. Undefined

46. _____ are a measure of time.
    a. Minutes0
    b. Thing
    c. Undefined
    d. Undefined

47. In mathematics and the mathematical sciences, a _____ is a fixed, but possibly unspecified, value. This is in contrast to a variable, which is not fixed.
    a. Thing
    b. Constant0
    c. Undefined
    d. Undefined

48. _____ is the ratio of the maximum width of the head to its maximum length i.e., in the horizontal plane, or front to back, sometimes multiplied by 100 for convenience.
    a. Thing
    b. Cephalic index0
    c. Undefined
    d. Undefined

49. In abstract algebra, _____ consists of sets with binary operations that satisfy certain axioms.
    a. Thing
    b. Grouping0
    c. Undefined
    d. Undefined

50. The word _____ is used in a variety of ways in mathematics.
    a. Index0
    b. Thing
    c. Undefined
    d. Undefined

51. A _____ is a unit of length, usually used to measure distance, in a number of different systems, including Imperial units, United States customary units and Norwegian/Swedish mil. Its size can vary from system to system, but in each is between 1 and 10 kilometers. In contemporary English contexts _____ refers to either:
    a. Mile0
    b. Thing
    c. Undefined
    d. Undefined

52. _____ is a unit of speed, expressing the number of international miles covered per hour.
    a. Thing
    b. Miles per hour0
    c. Undefined
    d. Undefined

53. _____ of a function of several variables is its derivative with respect to one of those variables with the others held constant as opposed to the total derivative, in which all variables are allowed to vary.
    a. Partial derivative0
    b. Thing
    c. Undefined
    d. Undefined

54. The _____ is a measurement of how a function changes when the values of its inputs change.
    a. Thing
    b. Derivative0
    c. Undefined
    d. Undefined

Chapter 8. Multivariable Calculus

55. _____ is often used to describe the measurement of the steepness, incline, gradient, or grade of a straight line. The _____ is defined as the ratio of the "rise" divided by the "run" between two points on a line, or in other words, the ratio of the altitude change to the horizontal distance between any two points on the line.
 a. Slope0 b. Thing
 c. Undefined d. Undefined

56. In trigonometry, the _____ is a function defined as $\tan x = \sin x / \cos x$. The function is so-named because it can be defined as the length of a certain segment of a _____ (in the geometric sense) to the unit circle. In plane geometry, a line is _____ to a curve, at some point, if both line and curve pass through the point with the same direction.
 a. Tangent0 b. Thing
 c. Undefined d. Undefined

57. _____ has two distinct but etymologically-related meanings: one in geometry and one in trigonometry.
 a. Thing b. Tangent line0
 c. Undefined d. Undefined

58. In calculus, the _____ is a formula for the derivative of the composite of two functions.
 a. Concept b. Chain rule0
 c. Undefined d. Undefined

59. In mathematics, the concept of a _____ tries to capture the intuitive idea of a geometrical one-dimensional and continuous object. A simple example is the circle.
 a. Thing b. Curve0
 c. Undefined d. Undefined

60. A pair of angles are _____ if the sum of their angles is 90°.
 a. Concept b. Complementary0
 c. Undefined d. Undefined

61. Acid _____ ratio measures the ability of a company to use its near cash or quick assets to immediately extinguish its current liabilities.
 a. Thing b. Test0
 c. Undefined d. Undefined

62. _____ is a free computer algebra system based on a 1982 version of Macsyma
 a. Maxima0 b. Thing
 c. Undefined d. Undefined

63. _____ are points in the domain of a function at which the function takes a largest value or smallest value, either within a given neighborhood or on the function domain in its entirety.
 a. Thing b. Maxima and minima0
 c. Undefined d. Undefined

64. In mathematics, maxima and _____, known collectively as extrema, are points in the domain of a function at which the function takes a largest value .

Chapter 8. Multivariable Calculus

a. Thing
b. Minima0
c. Undefined
d. Undefined

65. Deductive _____ is the kind of _____ in which the conclusion is necessitated by, or reached from, previously known facts (the premises).
    a. Reasoning0
    b. Thing
    c. Undefined
    d. Undefined

66. In mathematics, a _____ is a statement that can be proved on the basis of explicitly stated or previously agreed assumptions.
    a. Thing
    b. Theorem0
    c. Undefined
    d. Undefined

67. in mathematics, maxima and minima, known collectively as _____, are the largest value maximum or smallest value minimum, that a function takes in a point either within a given neighborhood or on the function domain in its entirety global extremum.
    a. Thing
    b. Extrema0
    c. Undefined
    d. Undefined

68. In mathematics, maxima and minima, known collectively as extrema, are the largest value maximum or smallest value minimum, that a function takes in a point either within a given neighborhood local _____ or on the function domain in its entirety global _____.
    a. Thing
    b. Extremum0
    c. Undefined
    d. Undefined

69. _____ Logic is a concept in traditional logic referring to a "type of immediate inference in which from a given proposition another proposition is inferred which has as its subject the predicate of the original proposition and as its predicate the subject of the original proposition (the quality of the proposition being retained)."
    a. Converse0
    b. Concept
    c. Undefined
    d. Undefined

70. _____ is a point on the domain of a function
    a. Thing
    b. Critical point0
    c. Undefined
    d. Undefined

71. A _____ of a number is the product of that number with any integer.
    a. Multiple0
    b. Thing
    c. Undefined
    d. Undefined

72. Generally, a _____ is a splitting of something into parts.
    a. Partition0
    b. Thing
    c. Undefined
    d. Undefined

73. _____ is the state of being greater than any finite real or natural number, however large.

a. Infinite0
b. Thing
c. Undefined
d. Undefined

74. In plane geometry, a _____ is a polygon with four equal sides, four right angles, and parallel opposite sides. In algebra, the _____ of a number is that number multiplied by itself.
   a. Thing
   b. Square0
   c. Undefined
   d. Undefined

75. A _____ is the result of the addition of a set of numbers. The numbers may be natural numbers, complex numbers, matrices, or still more complicated objects. An infinite _____ is a subtle procedure known as a series.
   a. Thing
   b. Sum0
   c. Undefined
   d. Undefined

76. _____, was an Italian mathematician and astronomer who created the calculus of variations which was later expanded by Weierstrass, solved the isoperimetrical problem on which the variational calculus is based in part.
   a. Joseph Louis Lagrange0
   b. Person
   c. Undefined
   d. Undefined

77. _____ are a method for finding the extrema of a function of several variables subject to one or more constraints: it is the basic tool in nonlinear constrained optimization.
   a. Lagrange multipliers0
   b. Thing
   c. Undefined
   d. Undefined

78. In mathematics, a _____ is a condition that a solution to an optimization problem must satisfy in order to be acceptable.
   a. Constraint0
   b. Thing
   c. Undefined
   d. Undefined

79. In mathematics, _____ expressions is used to reduce the expression into the lowest possible term.
   a. Simplifying0
   b. Thing
   c. Undefined
   d. Undefined

80. _____ is an economics theory, that refers to individuals or societies gaining the maximum amount out of the resources they have available to them.
   a. Thing
   b. Maximization0
   c. Undefined
   d. Undefined

81. The _____ or kilogramme is the SI base unit of mass. It is defined as being equal to the mass of the international prototype of the _____.
   a. Thing
   b. Kilogram0
   c. Undefined
   d. Undefined

82. In chemistry, a _____ is substance made by combining two or more different materials in such a way that no chemical reaction occurs.

Chapter 8. Multivariable Calculus

a. Thing
c. Undefined
b. Mixture0
d. Undefined

83. In regression analysis, _____, also known as ordinary _____ analysis is a method for linear regression that determines the values of unknown quantities in a statistical model by minimizing the sum of the residuals difference between the predicted and observed values squared.
   a. Least squares0
   c. Undefined
   b. Thing
   d. Undefined

84. The word _____ comes from the Latin word linearis, which means created by lines.
   a. Linear0
   c. Undefined
   b. Thing
   d. Undefined

85. A _____ is a first degree polynomial mathematical function of the form: f(x) = mx + b where m and b are real constants and x is a real variable.
   a. Thing
   c. Undefined
   b. Linear function0
   d. Undefined

86. _____ is a synonym for information.
   a. Thing
   c. Undefined
   b. Data0
   d. Undefined

87. In mathematics, a _____ set is the complement of a meager set. A meager set is one which is the countable union of nowhere dense sets.
   a. Residual0
   c. Undefined
   b. Thing
   d. Undefined

88. In mathematics, an _____, mean, or central tendency of a data set refers to a measure of the "middle" or "expected" value of the data set.
   a. Concept
   c. Undefined
   b. Average0
   d. Undefined

89. Mathematical _____ is used to represent ideas.
   a. Notation0
   c. Undefined
   b. Thing
   d. Undefined

90. _____ is the addition of a set of numbers; the result is their sum. The "numbers" to be summed may be natural numbers, complex numbers, matrices, or still more complicated objects. An infinite sum is a subtle procedure known as a series.
   a. Summation0
   c. Undefined
   b. Thing
   d. Undefined

91. An _____ is a combination of numbers, operators, grouping symbols and/or free variables and bound variables arranged in a meaningful way which can be evaluated..

a. Expression0
b. Thing
c. Undefined
d. Undefined

92. _____ is a concept that permeates much of inferential statistics and descriptive statistics. More properly, it is "the sum of the squared deviations".
    a. Thing
    b. Sum of squares0
    c. Undefined
    d. Undefined

93. In geographic information systems, a _____ comprises an entity with a geographic location, typically determined by points, arcs, or polygons. Carriageways and cadastres exemplify _____ data.
    a. Thing
    b. Feature0
    c. Undefined
    d. Undefined

94. _____ is a regression method that models the relationship between a dependent variable Y, independent variables Xp, and a random term à.
    a. Linear regression0
    b. Thing
    c. Undefined
    d. Undefined

95. In mathematics, a _____ is a mathematical statement which appears likely to be true, but has not been formally proven to be true under the rules of mathematical logic.
    a. Concept
    b. Conjecture0
    c. Undefined
    d. Undefined

96. In mathematics, a _____ is a polynomial equation of the second degree. The general form is $ax^2 + bx + c = 0$.
    a. Thing
    b. Quadratic equation0
    c. Undefined
    d. Undefined

97. A _____ is a statement or claimt that a particular event will occur in the future in more certain terms than a forecast.
    a. Prediction0
    b. Thing
    c. Undefined
    d. Undefined

98. In mathematics and elsewhere, the adjective _____ means fourth order, such as the function x4. A _____ number is a number which equals the fourth power of an integer.
    a. Quartic0
    b. Thing
    c. Undefined
    d. Undefined

99. In mathematics, _____ growth occurs when the growth rate of a function is always proportional to the function's current size.
    a. Exponential0
    b. Thing
    c. Undefined
    d. Undefined

100. _____ has many meanings, most of which simply .
    a. Power0
    b. Thing
    c. Undefined
    d. Undefined

Chapter 8. Multivariable Calculus

101. In mathematics, a _____ is a constant multiplicative factor of a certain object. The object can be such things as a variable, a vector, a function, etc. For example, the _____ of $9x^2$ is 9.
   a. Thing
   b. Coefficient0
   c. Undefined
   d. Undefined

102. In a mathematical proof or a syllogism, a _____ is a statement that is the logical consequence of preceding statements.
   a. Concept
   b. Conclusion0
   c. Undefined
   d. Undefined

103. In the scientific method, an _____ (Latin: ex-+-periri, "of (or from) trying"), is a set of actions and observations, performed in the context of solving a particular problem or question, in order to support or falsify a hypothesis or research concerning phenomena.
   a. Experiment0
   b. Thing
   c. Undefined
   d. Undefined

104. In mathematics, _____ refers to the rewriting of an expression into a simpler form.
   a. Thing
   b. Reduction0
   c. Undefined
   d. Undefined

105. _____ is a temperature scale named after the German physicist Daniel Gabriel _____ , who proposed it in 1724.
   a. Thing
   b. Fahrenheit0
   c. Undefined
   d. Undefined

106. A _____ is an equation in which each term is either a constant or the product of a constant times the first power of a variable.
   a. Thing
   b. Linear equation0
   c. Undefined
   d. Undefined

107. In mathematics, there are several meanings of _____ depending on the subject.
   a. Thing
   b. Degree0
   c. Undefined
   d. Undefined

108. _____ is a physical property of a system that underlies the common notions of hot and cold; something that is hotter has the greater _____.
   a. Thing
   b. Temperature0
   c. Undefined
   d. Undefined

109. In geometry, an _____ of a triangle is a straight line through a vertex and perpendicular to (i.e. forming a right angle with) the opposite side or an extension of the opposite side.
   a. Concept
   b. Altitude0
   c. Undefined
   d. Undefined

110. The _____ of a function is an extension of the concept of a sum, and are identified or found through the use of integration.

a. Integral0
b. Thing
c. Undefined
d. Undefined

111. _____, a field in mathematics, is the study of how functions change when their inputs change. The primary object of study in _____ is the derivative.
   a. Differential calculus0
   b. Thing
   c. Undefined
   d. Undefined

112. A _____ is a negotiable instrument instructing a financial institution to pay a specific amount of a specific currency from a specific demand account held in the maker/depositor's name with that institution. Both the maker and payee may be natural persons or legal entities.
   a. Check0
   b. Thing
   c. Undefined
   d. Undefined

113. _____ is a process of combining or accumulating. It may also refer to:
   a. Integration0
   b. Thing
   c. Undefined
   d. Undefined

114. An _____ of a function f is a function F whose derivative is equal to f, i.e., F' = f.
   a. Thing
   b. Antiderivative0
   c. Undefined
   d. Undefined

115. In calculus, the indefinite integral of a given function i.e. the set of all antiderivatives of the function is always written with a constant, the _____.
   a. Constant of integration0
   b. Thing
   c. Undefined
   d. Undefined

116. _____ is an extension of the concept of a sum.
   a. Thing
   b. Definite integral0
   c. Undefined
   d. Undefined

117. _____ in calculus is primitive or indefinite integral of a function f is a function F whose derivative is equal to f, i.e., F Œ = f. The process of solving for antiderivatives is _____
   a. Antidifferentiation0
   b. Thing
   c. Undefined
   d. Undefined

118. _____ is one of the most important functions in mathematics. A function commonly used to study growth and decay
   a. Thing
   b. Exponential function0
   c. Undefined
   d. Undefined

119. In mathematics, _____ geometry was the traditional name for the geometry of three-dimensional Euclidean space — for practical purposes the kind of space we live in.
   a. Solid0
   b. Thing
   c. Undefined
   d. Undefined

Chapter 8. Multivariable Calculus

120. A _____ is a deliberate process for transforming one or more inputs into one or more results.
 a. Calculation0
 b. Thing
 c. Undefined
 d. Undefined

121. In geometry, a _____ is defined as a quadrilateral where all four of its angles are right angles.
 a. Rectangle0
 b. Thing
 c. Undefined
 d. Undefined

122. _____ are cubes in which all sides are of the same length and all face perpendicular to each other including an atom at each corner of the unigt cell.
 a. Thing
 b. Cubic units0
 c. Undefined
 d. Undefined

123. A _____ signifies a point or points of probability on a subject e.g., the _____ of creativity, which allows for the formation of rule or norm or law by interpretation of the phenomena events that can be created.
 a. Thing
 b. Principle0
 c. Undefined
 d. Undefined

124. In sociology and biology a _____ is the collection of people or organisms of a particular species living in a given geographic area or space, usually measured by a census.
 a. Population0
 b. Thing
 c. Undefined
 d. Undefined

125. In mathematical analysis, _____ are objects which generalize functions and probability distributions.
 a. Distribution0
 b. Thing
 c. Undefined
 d. Undefined

126. A _____ is a function that assigns a number to subsets of a given set.
 a. Measure0
 b. Thing
 c. Undefined
 d. Undefined

127. In topology, the _____ are subsets S of a topological space X is the set of points which can be approached both from S and from the outside of S.
 a. Boundaries0
 b. Thing
 c. Undefined
 d. Undefined

128. In mathematics, a _____ is the end result of a division problem. It can also be expressed as the number of times the divisor divides into the dividend.
 a. Thing
 b. Quotient0
 c. Undefined
 d. Undefined

129. An _____ is a score derived from one of several different standardized tests attempting to measure intelligence.
 a. Intelligence Quotient0
 b. Thing
 c. Undefined
 d. Undefined

130. _____ is a statistical measure of the average length of survival of a living thing.

a. Thing
b. Life expectancy0
c. Undefined
d. Undefined

131. _____ is mass m per unit volume V.
a. Density0
b. Thing
c. Undefined
d. Undefined

132. _____ is an adjective usually refering to being in the centre.
a. Central0
b. Thing
c. Undefined
d. Undefined

133. In physics, _____ is an influence that may cause an object to accelerate. It may be experienced as a lift, a push, or a pull. The actual acceleration of the body is determined by the vector sum of all forces acting on it, known as net _____ or resultant _____.
a. Thing
b. Force0
c. Undefined
d. Undefined

134. The payment of _____ as remuneration for services rendered or products sold is a common way to reward sales people.
a. Thing
b. Commission0
c. Undefined
d. Undefined

135. In mathematics, a _____ number (or a _____) is a natural number that has exactly two (distinct) natural number divisors, which are 1 and the _____ number itself.
a. Thing
b. Prime0
c. Undefined
d. Undefined

136. _____ constitutes a broad family of algorithms for calculating the numerical value of a definite integral, and by extension, the term is also sometimes used to describe the numerical solution of differential equations.
a. Numerical integration0
b. Thing
c. Undefined
d. Undefined

137. In mathematics, a _____ is an expression that is constructed from one or more variables and constants, using only the operations of addition, subtraction, multiplication, and constant positive whole number exponents. is a _____. Note in particular that division by an expression containing a variable is not in general allowed in polynomials. [1]
a. Polynomial0
b. Thing
c. Undefined
d. Undefined

Chapter 9. Differential Equations

1. The _____ is a measurement of how a function changes when the values of its inputs change.
   a. Thing
   b. Derivative0
   c. Undefined
   d. Undefined

2. A _____ is traditionally an infinitesimally small change in a variable.
   a. Thing
   b. Differential0
   c. Undefined
   d. Undefined

3. A _____ is a mathematical equation for an unknown function of one or several variables which relates the values of the function itself and of its derivatives of various orders.
   a. Differential equation0
   b. Thing
   c. Undefined
   d. Undefined

4. The mathematical concept of a _____ expresses the intuitive idea of deterministic dependence between two quantities, one of which is viewed as primary and the other as secondary. A _____ then is a way to associate a unique output for each input of a specified type, for example, a real number or an element of a given set.
   a. Thing
   b. Function0
   c. Undefined
   d. Undefined

5. A _____ is a symbolic representation denoting a quantity or expression. It often represents an "unknown" quantity that has the potential to change.
   a. Variable0
   b. Thing
   c. Undefined
   d. Undefined

6. In mathematics, an _____ is any of the arguments, i.e. "inputs", to a function. Thus if we have a function f(x), then x is a _____.
   a. Independent variable0
   b. Thing
   c. Undefined
   d. Undefined

7. In geometry, a line _____ is a part of a line that is bounded by two end points, and contains every point on the line between its end points.
   a. Segment0
   b. Concept
   c. Undefined
   d. Undefined

8. _____ is often used to describe the measurement of the steepness, incline, gradient, or grade of a straight line. The _____ is defined as the ratio of the "rise" divided by the "run" between two points on a line, or in other words, the ratio of the altitude change to the horizontal distance between any two points on the line.
   a. Thing
   b. Slope0
   c. Undefined
   d. Undefined

9. A _____ is a graphical tool to qualitatively visualize, or aid in numerical approximation of, solutions to differential equations.
   a. Thing
   b. Slope field0
   c. Undefined
   d. Undefined

Chapter 9. Differential Equations

10. In trigonometry, the _____ is a function defined as $\tan x = \sin x / \cos x$. The function is so-named because it can be defined as the length of a certain segment of a _____ (in the geometric sense) to the unit circle. In plane geometry, a line is _____ to a curve, at some point, if both line and curve pass through the point with the same direction.
    a. Tangent0
    b. Thing
    c. Undefined
    d. Undefined

11. A _____ is a part of a line that is bounded by two end points, and contains every point on the line between its end points.
    a. Thing
    b. Line segment0
    c. Undefined
    d. Undefined

12. _____ has two distinct but etymologically-related meanings: one in geometry and one in trigonometry.
    a. Tangent line0
    b. Thing
    c. Undefined
    d. Undefined

13. _____ are external two-dimensional outlines, with the appearance or configuration of some thing - in contrast to the matter or content or substance of which it is composed.
    a. Shapes0
    b. Thing
    c. Undefined
    d. Undefined

14. In mathematics and the mathematical sciences, a _____ is a fixed, but possibly unspecified, value. This is in contrast to a variable, which is not fixed.
    a. Thing
    b. Constant0
    c. Undefined
    d. Undefined

15. An _____ is when two lines intersect somewhere on a plane creating a right angle at intersection
    a. Thing
    b. Axes0
    c. Undefined
    d. Undefined

16. Initial objects are also called _____, and terminal objects are also called final.
    a. Thing
    b. Coterminal0
    c. Undefined
    d. Undefined

17. In mathematics, the concept of a _____ tries to capture the intuitive idea of a geometrical one-dimensional and continuous object. A simple example is the circle.
    a. Thing
    b. Curve0
    c. Undefined
    d. Undefined

18. In mathematics, _____ are the intuitive idea of a geometrical one-dimensional and continuous object.
    a. Curves0
    b. Thing
    c. Undefined
    d. Undefined

19. In mathematics, in the field of differential equations, an initial value problem is a differential equation together with specified value, called the _____, of the unknown function at a given point in the domain of the solution.

a. Initial condition0 b. Thing
c. Undefined d. Undefined

20. In statistics, a _____ measure is one which is measuring what is supposed to measure.
    a. Valid0 b. Thing
    c. Undefined d. Undefined

21. A _____ is a deliberate process for transforming one or more inputs into one or more results.
    a. Thing b. Calculation0
    c. Undefined d. Undefined

22. An _____ is a combination of numbers, operators, grouping symbols and/or free variables and bound variables arranged in a meaningful way which can be evaluated..
    a. Expression0 b. Thing
    c. Undefined d. Undefined

23. _____ is to give an equation R(x,y) = S(x,y) that at least in part has the same graph as y = f(x).
    a. Implicit differentiation0 b. Thing
    c. Undefined d. Undefined

24. _____, a field in mathematics, is the study of how functions change when their inputs change. The primary object of study in _____ is the derivative.
    a. Thing b. Differential calculus0
    c. Undefined d. Undefined

25. In mathematics, a _____ is the result of multiplying, or an expression that identifies factors to be multiplied.
    a. Product0 b. Thing
    c. Undefined d. Undefined

26. In business, particularly accounting, a _____ is the time intervals that the accounts, statement, payments, or other calculations cover.
    a. Period0 b. Thing
    c. Undefined d. Undefined

27. In economics, economic _____ is simply a state of the world where economic forces are balanced and in the absence of external influences the values of economic variables will not change.
    a. Thing b. Equilibrium0
    c. Undefined d. Undefined

28. _____ is the price at which the quantity demanded of a good or service is equal to the quantity supplied.
    a. Thing b. Equilibrium price0
    c. Undefined d. Undefined

29. _____ Any process by which a specified characteristic usually amplitude of the output of a device is prevented from exceeding a predetermined value.

a. Limiting0
b. Thing
c. Undefined
d. Undefined

30. _____ is the state of being greater than any finite number, however large.
a. Thing
b. Infinity0
c. Undefined
d. Undefined

31. _____ are the basic objects of study in graph theory. Informally speaking, a graph is a set of objects called points, nodes, or vertices connected by links called lines or edges.
a. Thing
b. Graphs0
c. Undefined
d. Undefined

32. A _____ is a special kind of ratio, indicating a relationship between two measurements with different units, such as miles to gallons or cents to pounds.
a. Thing
b. Rate0
c. Undefined
d. Undefined

33. In mathematics, two quantities are called _____ if they vary in such a way that one of the quantities is a constant multiple of the other, or equivalently if they have a constant ratio.
a. Proportional0
b. Thing
c. Undefined
d. Undefined

34. _____ is a physical property of a system that underlies the common notions of hot and cold; something that is hotter has the greater _____.
a. Temperature0
b. Thing
c. Undefined
d. Undefined

35. U.S. liquid _____ is legally defined as 231 cubic inches, and is equal to 3.785411784 litres or abotu 0.13368 cubic feet. This is the most common definition of a _____. The U.S. fluid ounce is defined as 1/128 of a U.S. _____.
a. Gallon0
b. Thing
c. Undefined
d. Undefined

36. _____ is a a point on a curve at which the tangent crosses the curve itself.
a. Thing
b. Inflection point0
c. Undefined
d. Undefined

37. _____ is a kind of property which exists as magnitude or multitude. It is among the basic classes of things along with quality, substance, change, and relation.
a. Amount0
b. Thing
c. Undefined
d. Undefined

38. A _____ function is a function for which, intuitively, small changes in the input result in small changes in the output.

a. Event
b. Continuous0
c. Undefined
d. Undefined

39. In sociology and biology a _____ is the collection of people or organisms of a particular species living in a given geographic area or space, usually measured by a census.
   a. Population0
   b. Thing
   c. Undefined
   d. Undefined

40. _____ is change in population over time, and can be quantified as the change in the number of individuals in a population per unit time.
   a. Thing
   b. Population growth0
   c. Undefined
   d. Undefined

41. Pierre François _____ was a mathematician and a doctor in number theory from the University of Ghent in 1825.
   a. Verhulst0
   b. Person
   c. Undefined
   d. Undefined

42. The _____ of a function is an extension of the concept of a sum, and are identified or found through the use of integration.
   a. Thing
   b. Integral0
   c. Undefined
   d. Undefined

43. _____ is a process of combining or accumulating. It may also refer to:
   a. Integration0
   b. Thing
   c. Undefined
   d. Undefined

44. An _____ of a function f is a function F whose derivative is equal to f, i.e., F' = f.
   a. Antiderivative0
   b. Thing
   c. Undefined
   d. Undefined

45. In mathematics, _____ growth occurs when the growth rate of a function is always proportional to the function's current size.
   a. Exponential0
   b. Thing
   c. Undefined
   d. Undefined

46. In mathematics, the _____ (or modulus) of a real number is its numerical value without regard to its sign.
   a. Absolute value0
   b. Thing
   c. Undefined
   d. Undefined

47. Equivalence is the condition of being _____ or essentially equal.
   a. Thing
   b. Equivalent0
   c. Undefined
   d. Undefined

48. _____ is one of the most important functions in mathematics. A function commonly used to study growth and decay

a. Exponential function0
b. Thing
c. Undefined
d. Undefined

49. The _____ of a solid object is the three-dimensional concept of how much space it occupies, often quantified numerically.
   a. Volume0
   b. Thing
   c. Undefined
   d. Undefined

50. In mathematics, _____ occurs when the growth rate of a function is always proportional to the function's current size.
   a. Thing
   b. Exponential growth0
   c. Undefined
   d. Undefined

51. In mathematics, the _____ of two sets A and B is the set that contains all elements of A that also belong to B (or equivalently, all elements of B that also belong to A), but no other elements.
   a. Thing
   b. Intersection0
   c. Undefined
   d. Undefined

52. A _____ is a numeral used to indicate a count. The most common use of the word today is to name the part of a fraction that tells the number or count of equal parts.
   a. Thing
   b. Numerator0
   c. Undefined
   d. Undefined

53. A _____ is the part of a fraction that tells how many equal parts make up a whole, and which is used in the name of the fraction: "halves", "thirds", "fourths" or "quarters", "fifths" and so on.
   a. Concept
   b. Denominator0
   c. Undefined
   d. Undefined

54. In astronomy, geography, geometry and related sciences and contexts, a plane is said to be _____ at a given point if it is locally perpendicular to the gradient of the gravity field, i.e., with the direction of the gravitational force at that point.
   a. Horizontal0
   b. Thing
   c. Undefined
   d. Undefined

55. _____ is a synonym for information.
   a. Data0
   b. Thing
   c. Undefined
   d. Undefined

56. _____ is the fee paid on borrowed money.
   a. Thing
   b. Interest0
   c. Undefined
   d. Undefined

57. _____ interest refers to the fact that whenever interest is calculated, it is based not only on the original principal, but also on any unpaid interest that has been added to the principal.
   a. Thing
   b. Compound0
   c. Undefined
   d. Undefined

Chapter 9. Differential Equations 117

58. _____ refers to the fact that whenever interest is calculated, it is based not only on the original principal, but also on any unpaid interest that has been added to the principal. The more frequently interest is compounded, the faster the balance grows.
    a. Compound interest0
    b. Concept
    c. Undefined
    d. Undefined

59. In physics, a _____ may refer to the scalar _____ or to the vector _____.
    a. Potential0
    b. Thing
    c. Undefined
    d. Undefined

60. A _____ is an individual or household that purchases and uses goods and services generated within the economy.
    a. Consumer0
    b. Thing
    c. Undefined
    d. Undefined

61. Sir Isaac _____, was an English physicist, mathematician, astronomer, natural philosopher, and alchemist, regarded by many as the greatest figure in the history of science
    a. Person
    b. Newton0
    c. Undefined
    d. Undefined

62. The word _____ comes from the Latin word linearis, which means created by lines.
    a. Linear0
    b. Thing
    c. Undefined
    d. Undefined

63. In epidemiology, an _____ is a disease that appears as new cases in a given human population, during a given period, at a rate that substantially exceeds with is "expected," based on recent experience.
    a. Thing
    b. Epidemic0
    c. Undefined
    d. Undefined

64. The _____ of a mathematical object is its size: a property by which it can be larger or smaller than other objects of the same kind; in technical terms, an ordering of the class of objects to which it belongs.
    a. Thing
    b. Magnitude0
    c. Undefined
    d. Undefined

65. A _____ is a function that assigns a number to subsets of a given set.
    a. Thing
    b. Measure0
    c. Undefined
    d. Undefined

66. The _____ governs the differentiation of products of differentiable functions.
    a. Thing
    b. Product rule0
    c. Undefined
    d. Undefined

67. A _____ is 360° or 2δ radians.
    a. Thing
    b. Turn0
    c. Undefined
    d. Undefined

Chapter 9. Differential Equations

68. _____ is a function that is chosen to facilitate the solving of a given ordinary differential equation.Consider an ordinary differential equation of the form
   a. Thing
   b. Integrating factor0
   c. Undefined
   d. Undefined

69. _____ the expected value of a random variable displays the average or central value of the variable.It is a summary value of the distribution of the variable.
   a. Determining0
   b. Thing
   c. Undefined
   d. Undefined

70. _____ is a notation for writing numbers that is often used by scientists and mathematicians to make it easier to write large and small numbers.
   a. Scientific notation0
   b. Thing
   c. Undefined
   d. Undefined

71. In calculus, the indefinite integral of a given function i.e. the set of all antiderivatives of the function is always written with a constant, the _____.
   a. Constant of integration0
   b. Thing
   c. Undefined
   d. Undefined

72. In mathematics, a _____ of a complex-valued function f is a member x of the domain of f such that f(x) vanishes at x, that is, x : f (x) = 0.
   a. Thing
   b. Root0
   c. Undefined
   d. Undefined

73. A _____ is an equation in which each term is either a constant or the product of a constant times the first power of a variable.
   a. Thing
   b. Linear equation0
   c. Undefined
   d. Undefined

74. In economics, supply and _____ describe market relations between prospective sellers and buyers of a good.
   a. Demand0
   b. Thing
   c. Undefined
   d. Undefined

75. _____ is a function that extends the concept of an ordinary sum
   a. Thing
   b. Integrand0
   c. Undefined
   d. Undefined

76. A _____ is a negotiable instrument instructing a financial institution to pay a specific amount of a specific currency from a specific demand account held in the maker/depositor's name with that institution. Both the maker and payee may be natural persons or legal entities.
   a. Thing
   b. Check0
   c. Undefined
   d. Undefined

77. A _____ is a form of collective investment that pools money from many investors and invests their money in stocks, bonds, short-term money market instruments, and/or other securities.

Chapter 9. Differential Equations

a. Thing
c. Undefined
b. Mutual fund0
d. Undefined

78. _____ or investing is a term with several closely-related meanings in business management, finance and economics, related to saving or deferring consumption.
   a. Thing
   c. Undefined
   b. Investment0
   d. Undefined

79. _____ are objects, characters, or other concrete representations of ideas, concepts, or other abstractions.
   a. Thing
   c. Undefined
   b. Symbols0
   d. Undefined

80. In botany, _____ are above-ground plant organs specialized for photosynthesis. Their characteristics are typically analyzed by using Fiobonacci's sequences.
   a. Leaves0
   c. Undefined
   b. Thing
   d. Undefined

81. A _____ y_s of an ordinary differential equation is a solution that is tangent to every solution from the family of general solutions.
   a. Thing
   c. Undefined
   b. Singular solution0
   d. Undefined

82. _____ is a term used in accounting, economics and finance with reference to the fact that assets with finite lives lose value over time.
   a. Depreciation0
   c. Undefined
   b. Thing
   d. Undefined

83. In geometry, a _____ (Greek words diairo = divide and metro = measure) of a circle is any straight line segment that passes through the centre and whose endpoints are on the circular boundary, or, in more modern usage, the length of such a line segment. When using the word in the more modern sense, one speaks of the _____ rather than a _____, because all diameters of a circle have the same length. This length is twice the radius. The _____ of a circle is also the longest chord that the circle has.
   a. Diameter0
   c. Undefined
   b. Thing
   d. Undefined

84. In Euclidean geometry, a uniform _____ is a linear transformation that enlargers or diminishes objects, and whose _____ factor is the same in all directions. This is also called homothethy.
   a. Scale0
   c. Undefined
   b. Thing
   d. Undefined

85. A _____ is a set of numbers that designate location in a given reference system, such as x,y in a planar _____ system or an x,y,z in a three-dimensional _____ system.
   a. Coordinate0
   c. Undefined
   b. Thing
   d. Undefined

86. In plane geometry, a _____ is a polygon with four equal sides, four right angles, and parallel opposite sides. In algebra, the _____ of a number is that number multiplied by itself.
   a. Square0
   b. Thing
   c. Undefined
   d. Undefined

87. In mathematics, a _____ of a number x is a number r such that $r^2 = x$, or in words, a number r whose square (the result of multiplying the number by itself) is x.
   a. Thing
   b. Square root0
   c. Undefined
   d. Undefined

88. In mathematics, a _____ is a two-dimensional manifold or surface that is perfectly flat.
   a. Plane0
   b. Thing
   c. Undefined
   d. Undefined

89. In mathematics, a _____ is an ordered list of objects. Like a set, it contains members, also called elements or terms, and the number of terms is called the length of the _____. Unlike a set, order matters, and the exact same elements can appear multiple times at different positions in the _____.
   a. Sequence0
   b. Thing
   c. Undefined
   d. Undefined

90. _____ is a method of defining functions in which the function being defined is applied within its own definition. The term is also used more generally to describe a process of repeating objects in a self-similar way.
   a. Recursion0
   b. Thing
   c. Undefined
   d. Undefined

91. Leonhard _____ was a pioneering Swiss mathematician and physicist, who spent most of his life in Russia and Germany.
   a. Euler0
   b. Person
   c. Undefined
   d. Undefined

92. _____ is a mathematical science pertaining to the collection, analysis, interpretation or explanation, and presentation of data. It is applicable to a wide variety of academic disciplines, from the physical and social sciences to the humanities.
   a. Statistics0
   b. Thing
   c. Undefined
   d. Undefined

Chapter 10. Taylor Polynomials and Infinite Series

1. _____ or arithmetics (from the Greek word áñééìüò = number) in common usage is a branch of (or the forerunner of) mathematics which records elementary properties of certain operations on numerals, though in usage by professional mathematicians, it often is treated as a synonym for number theory.
   a. Arithmetic10
   b. ACTRAN
   c. Undefined
   d. Undefined

2. A _____ is a class of simple functions where they are constructed using only multiplication and addition of terms.
   a. 15 theorem
   b. Polynomial10
   c. Undefined
   d. Undefined

3. The most important measure of central tendency, and one of the basic building blocks of all statistical analysis, is the arithmetic <U>mean.</U> It is simply the sum of all the set of values divided by the number of values involved. It can also be called the average.
   a. Mean10
   b. 15 theorem
   c. Undefined
   d. Undefined

4. The probability of correctly rejecting a false Ho is referred to as _____.
   a. Power10
   b. 15 theorem
   c. Undefined
   d. Undefined

5. The word _____ can have three meanings: In _____ theory, a _____ is an abstract object consisting of vertices (or nodes) and edges (or arcs) between pairs of vertices. The _____ of a function f : X ¨ Y is the set of all pairs (x,f(x)) The _____ of a relation, a generalisation of the _____ of a function.
   a. 15 theorem
   b. Graph10
   c. Undefined
   d. Undefined

6. _____, or less commonly, denary, usually refers to the base 10 numeral system.
   a. Decimal10
   b. 15 theorem
   c. Undefined
   d. Undefined

7. A <U>horizontal line </U>goes from left to right or from East to West.
   a. Horizontal line10
   b. 15 theorem
   c. Undefined
   d. Undefined

8. A measure of variability, the _____ is the distance from the lowest to the highest score.
   a. Range10
   b. 15 theorem
   c. Undefined
   d. Undefined

9. The _____ or central tendency of a list of n numbers. All the values are added together and then divided by the number of values. It is also call the mean..
   a. ACTRAN
   b. Average10
   c. Undefined
   d. Undefined

10. An <U>equation</U> is represented by two expressions that have the same value.
    a. Equation10
    b. ACTRAN
    c. Undefined
    d. Undefined

11. In a large distribution of data it is often easier to understand the data if it is grouped into intervals where each _____ can contain more than one data value. Distributions are often reduced to 10 to 20 intervals.
   a. ACTRAN
   b. Interval10
   c. Undefined
   d. Undefined

12. An _____ is an action applied to numbers or other entities to produce a well-defined result.
   a. Operation10
   b. ACTRAN
   c. Undefined
   d. Undefined

13. A quadrilateral with 4 equal sides and all right angles is called a <U>square.</U>
   a. 15 theorem
   b. Square10
   c. Undefined
   d. Undefined

14. Addition (or summation) is one of the basic operations of arithmetic. In its simplest form, addition combines two numbers, the augend and addend, into a single number, the _____. Adding more numbers can be viewed as repeated addition. (Repeated addition of the number one is the most basic form of counting.) By extension, the addition of zero numbers, one number, or infinitely many numbers can be defined.
   a. 15 theorem
   b. Sum10
   c. Undefined
   d. Undefined

15. A _____ is the relationship between two quantities. It is expressed as the quotient of two numbers, or as two numbers separated by a colon (pronounced "to"). A number that can be written as a _____ of two integers is a rational number.
   a. Ratio10
   b. 15 theorem
   c. Undefined
   d. Undefined

16. A <U>point </U>is an undefined term. We usually represent this by a dot, but a _____ actually has no dimension. A capital letter names any _____.
   a. Point10
   b. 15 theorem
   c. Undefined
   d. Undefined

17. A _____ is a well-defined collection of objects considered as a whole.
   a. Set10
   b. 15 theorem
   c. Undefined
   d. Undefined

18. The outcome of a trial is called the _____.
   a. Event10
   b. ACTRAN
   c. Undefined
   d. Undefined

19. The bottom part of any fraction represents the number of pieces in one whole unit. This bottom part is called the <U>denominator.</U>
   a. 15 theorem
   b. Denominator10
   c. Undefined
   d. Undefined

20. The top part of the fraction is called the <U>numerator</U>. It could also be called the dividend, but _____ is preferred.

Chapter 10. Taylor Polynomials and Infinite Series

a. 15 theorem
b. Numerator10
c. Undefined
d. Undefined

21. _____ (or summation) is one of the basic operations of arithmetic. In its simplest form, _____ combines two numbers, the augend and addend, into a single number, the sum.
   a. Addition10
   b. ACTRAN
   c. Undefined
   d. Undefined

22. A number that does not change in value in a given situation is a _____.
   a. 15 theorem
   b. Constant10
   c. Undefined
   d. Undefined

23. An _____ combines numbers, operators, and/or variables but contains no equal or inequality sign.
   a. Expression10
   b. ACTRAN
   c. Undefined
   d. Undefined

24. <U>Multiplication</U> is a quick way of adding identical numbers. For example, the sum 7 + 7 + 7 can be found by multiplying 3 times 7. This model is reflected in the use of the word times as a synonym for multiplied by. The resuult of multiplying numbers is called a product. The numbers being multiplied are called factors.
   a. Multiplication10
   b. 15 theorem
   c. Undefined
   d. Undefined

25. A _____ is a number or variable, or the product or quotient of a number or variable.
   a. 15 theorem
   b. Term10
   c. Undefined
   d. Undefined

26. When a divisor does not divide into the dividend evenly, the left over number is called the <U>remainder.</U> In most cases, we would write this as a fraction by putting the _____ over the divisor.
   a. Remainder10
   b. 15 theorem
   c. Undefined
   d. Undefined

27. An _____ is an indication of the value of an unknown quantity based on observed data. More formally, an _____ is the particular value of an estimator that is obtained from a particular sample of data and used to indicate the value of a parameter.
   a. Estimate10
   b. ACTRAN
   c. Undefined
   d. Undefined

28. Any time one number is on the left side of another number on a number line, the first number is <U>less than </U>the second number. The symbol for this is <.
   a. Less than10
   b. 15 theorem
   c. Undefined
   d. Undefined

29. The _____ of a number is the distance between zero and the number on the lnumber line.
   a. Absolute value10
   b. ACTRAN
   c. Undefined
   d. Undefined

30. The highest number in a list of values is called the <U>maximum.</U>
   a. 15 theorem
   b. Maximum10
   c. Undefined
   d. Undefined

31. In statistics an arrangement of values of a variable showing their observed or theoretical frequency of occurrence is called a _____.
   a. 15 theorem
   b. Distribution10
   c. Undefined
   d. Undefined

32. A _____ is an undefined term. However, it is often thought of as a series of points. A _____ has one dimension - length. A _____ is either named by a lower case letter or by two points on the _____.
   a. 15 theorem
   b. Line10
   c. Undefined
   d. Undefined

33. <U>Twice</U> means to multiply by 2.
   a. Twice10
   b. 15 theorem
   c. Undefined
   d. Undefined

34. When a given number is the product of another number by itself, the another number is called the <U>square root</U>. Ex: 25 = 5 x 5 so 5 is the _____ of 25.
   a. Square root10
   b. 15 theorem
   c. Undefined
   d. Undefined

35. <U>Degrees</U> are used to measure the size of angles. A circle has 360 _____ in it.
   a. 15 theorem
   b. Degrees10
   c. Undefined
   d. Undefined

36. _____ is the process by which sample data are used to indicate the value of an unknown quantity in a population.
   a. ACTRAN
   b. Estimation10
   c. Undefined
   d. Undefined

37. A _____ is the end result of a division problem. For example, in the problem 6 ÷ 3, the _____ would be 2, while 6 would be called the dividend, and 3 the divisor
   a. Quotient10
   b. 15 theorem
   c. Undefined
   d. Undefined

Chapter 11. Probability and Calculus

1. The word _____ can have three meanings: In _____ theory, a _____ is an abstract object consisting of vertices (or nodes) and edges (or arcs) between pairs of vertices. The _____ of a function f : X ¨ Y is the set of all pairs (x,f(x)) The _____ of a relation, a generalisation of the _____ of a function.
   a. 15 theorem
   b. Graph11
   c. Undefined
   d. Undefined

2. In a large distribution of data it is often easier to understand the data if it is grouped into intervals where each _____ can contain more than one data value. Distributions are often reduced to 10 to 20 intervals.
   a. ACTRAN
   b. Interval11
   c. Undefined
   d. Undefined

3. At times we must contend with variables that assume a large number of values. In this case it is typical to create _____ of values of the variable and then make a frequency tally of the number of observations falling within each interval. As is the case with any data reduction technique, detail is lost.
   a. Intervals11
   b. ACTRAN
   c. Undefined
   d. Undefined

4. An _____ is an indication of the value of an unknown quantity based on observed data. More formally, an _____ is the particular value of an estimator that is obtained from a particular sample of data and used to indicate the value of a parameter.
   a. Estimate11
   b. ACTRAN
   c. Undefined
   d. Undefined

5. An _____ is an action applied to numbers or other entities to produce a well-defined result.
   a. Operation11
   b. ACTRAN
   c. Undefined
   d. Undefined

6. _____ is a central branch of mathematics, developed from algebra and geometry, and built on two major complementary ideas, differential _____ and integral _____.
   a. 15 theorem
   b. Calculus11
   c. Undefined
   d. Undefined

7. A _____ provides a quantitative description of the likely occurrence of a particular event. _____ is conventionally expressed on a scale from 0 to 1; a rare event has a _____ close to 0, a very common event has a _____ close to 1. _____ is calculated as the ratio of the number of favorable events to the total number of possible events.
   a. Probability11
   b. 15 theorem
   c. Undefined
   d. Undefined

8. A number that does not change in value in a given situation is a _____.
   a. 15 theorem
   b. Constant11
   c. Undefined
   d. Undefined

9. A _____, also referred to as a universe, is any well-defined collection of things. By well-defined we mean that the members of the _____ are spelled out, or an unequivocal statement is made as to which things belong in it and which do not.

a. Population11
b. 15 theorem
c. Undefined
d. Undefined

10. _____, the height of the curve for a given value of X; closely related to the probability of an observation in an interval around X.
   a. 15 theorem
   b. Density11
   c. Undefined
   d. Undefined

11. In statistics an arrangement of values of a variable showing their observed or theoretical frequency of occurrence is called a _____.
   a. Distribution11
   b. 15 theorem
   c. Undefined
   d. Undefined

12. An _____ is any process or study, which results in the collection of data, the outcome of which is unknown. In statistics, the term is usually restricted to situations in which the researcher has control over some of the conditions under which the _____ takes place.
   a. ACTRAN
   b. Experiment11
   c. Undefined
   d. Undefined

13. The number of times a particular score or observation occurs is its _____.
   a. 15 theorem
   b. Frequency11
   c. Undefined
   d. Undefined

14. An _____ is the result of an experiment or other situation involving uncertainty.
   a. ACTRAN
   b. Outcome11
   c. Undefined
   d. Undefined

15. _____ are characteristics or properties of an object that can take on one or more different values.
   a. Variables11
   b. 15 theorem
   c. Undefined
   d. Undefined

16. A _____ is one, which takes an infinite number of possible values. Continuous random variables are usually measurements. Examples include height, weight, the amount of sugar in an orange, the time required to run a mile.
   a. Continuous Random Variable11
   b. 15 theorem
   c. Undefined
   d. Undefined

17. _____ are intuitively defined as numbers that are in one-to-one correspondence with the points on an infinite line—the number line. The term "real number" is a retronym coined in response to "imaginary number" _____ may be rational or irrational; algebraic or transcendental; and positive, negative, or zero _____ measure continuous quantities. They may in theory be expressed by decimal fractions that have an infinite sequence of digits to the right of the decimal point; these are often (mis-)represented in the same form as 324.823211247... (where the three dots express that there would still be more digits to come, no matter how many more might be added at the end).
   a. Real numbers11
   b. 15 theorem
   c. Undefined
   d. Undefined

18. A _____ is a well-defined collection of objects considered as a whole.

Chapter 11. Probability and Calculus

a. Set11
b. 15 theorem
c. Undefined
d. Undefined

19. Addition (or summation) is one of the basic operations of arithmetic. In its simplest form, addition combines two numbers, the augend and addend, into a single number, the _____. Adding more numbers can be viewed as repeated addition. (Repeated addition of the number one is the most basic form of counting.) By extension, the addition of zero numbers, one number, or infinitely many numbers can be defined.
    a. 15 theorem
    b. Sum11
    c. Undefined
    d. Undefined

20. _____ (or summation) is one of the basic operations of arithmetic. In its simplest form, _____ combines two numbers, the augend and addend, into a single number, the sum.
    a. ACTRAN
    b. Addition11
    c. Undefined
    d. Undefined

21. A _____ is one which may take on only a countable number of distinct values such as 0,1,2,3,4,....... Discrete random variables are usually (but not necessarily) counts. If a random variable can take only a finite number of distinct values, then it must be discrete. Examples of discrete random variables include the number of children in a family, the Friday night attendance at a cinema, the number of patients in a doctor's surgery, the number of defective light bulbs in a box of ten.
    a. 15 theorem
    b. Discrete Random Variable11
    c. Undefined
    d. Undefined

22. The outcome of an experiment need not be a number, for example, the outcome when a coin is tossed can be 'heads' or 'tails'. However, we often want to represent outcomes as numbers. A _____ is a function that associates a unique numerical value with every outcome of an experiment. The value of the random
    a. 15 theorem
    b. Random Variable11
    c. Undefined
    d. Undefined

23. The very fact that we are measuring objects with respect to some characteristic implies that the objects differ in that characteristic; or stated in another way, that the characteristic can take on a number of different values. These properties or characteristics of an object that can assume two or more different values are referred to as a _____.
    a. Variable11
    b. 15 theorem
    c. Undefined
    d. Undefined

24. The _____ of a continuous random variable is a function, which can be integrated to obtain the probability that the random variable takes a value in a given interval.
    a. 15 theorem
    b. Probability Density Function11
    c. Undefined
    d. Undefined

25. A measure of variability, the _____ is the distance from the lowest to the highest score.
    a. 15 theorem
    b. Range11
    c. Undefined
    d. Undefined

26. The _____ provides the probability value associated with each point in a distribution of scores. The value indicates the likelihood of obtaining such a value from the distribution.

Chapter 11. Probability and Calculus

    a. 15 theorem
    b. Probability distribution11
    c. Undefined
    d. Undefined

27. A <U>point </U>is an undefined term. We usually represent this by a dot, but a _____ actually has no dimension. A capital letter names any _____.
    a. Point11
    b. 15 theorem
    c. Undefined
    d. Undefined

28. All random variables (discrete and continuous) have a _____. It is a function giving the probability that the random variable X is less than or equal to x, for every value x.
    a. Cumulative Distribution Function11
    b. 15 theorem
    c. Undefined
    d. Undefined

29. An <U>equation</U> is represented by two expressions that have the same value.
    a. ACTRAN
    b. Equation11
    c. Undefined
    d. Undefined

30. _____, or less commonly, denary, usually refers to the base 10 numeral system.
    a. 15 theorem
    b. Decimal11
    c. Undefined
    d. Undefined

31. A _____ is an undefined term. However, it is often thought of as a series of points. A _____ has one dimension - length. A _____ is either named by a lower case letter or by two points on the _____.
    a. Line11
    b. 15 theorem
    c. Undefined
    d. Undefined

32. A summary value that would suggest a typical or representative observation of a distribution of data, is a measure of _____ or location; that is, a value at which the observations tend to center.
    a. Central tendency11
    b. 15 theorem
    c. Undefined
    d. Undefined

33. By _____ we mean collecting observations made upon our environment -- observations, which are the results of measurements using clocks, balances, measuring rods, counting operations, or other objectively defined measuring instruments or procedures. _____ may mean simply counting the number of times a particular property occurs.
    a. Data11
    b. 15 theorem
    c. Undefined
    d. Undefined

34. A _____ refers to the distance or difference between any score in a distribution of data from the mean.
    a. 15 theorem
    b. Deviation11
    c. Undefined
    d. Undefined

35. The degree to which individual data points are distributed around the mean is referred to as _____.
    a. Dispersion11
    b. 15 theorem
    c. Undefined
    d. Undefined

36. The long-range average of a statistic over repeated samples is the _____.

a. ACTRAN
b. Expected value11
c. Undefined
d. Undefined

37. The most important measure of central tendency, and one of the basic building blocks of all statistical analysis, is the arithmetic <U>mean.</U> It is simply the sum of all the set of values divided by the number of values involved. It can also be called the average.
a. 15 theorem
b. Mean11
c. Undefined
d. Undefined

38. A measure of central tendency, the _____, corresponds to the point having 50% of the observations below it when observations are arranged in numerical order. The _____ assumes at least an interval level of measurement. For a symmetric distribution such as the normal distribution, the _____ is the same as the mean. For a distribution which is skewed to the right, the _____ is typically smaller than the mean or when skewed to the left, the _____ is smaller.
a. 15 theorem
b. Median11
c. Undefined
d. Undefined

39. A _____ is a concrete example of an item or a specification against which all others may be measured. For example, there are "primary standards" for length, mass (see Kilogram standard), and other units of measure, kept by laboratories and standards organizations.
a. 15 theorem
b. Standard11
c. Undefined
d. Undefined

40. A measure of variability in a distribution, the _____ is the square root of the variance. The _____ measures the variability of scores around the mean: the standardized difference. It is the square root of the mean square error.
a. Standard deviation11
b. 15 theorem
c. Undefined
d. Undefined

41. The _____ is the a statistic which measures how spread out or dispersed a set of data is. It is The value calculated will always be greater than or equal to zero, with larger values corresponding to data which is more spread out. If all data values are identical, the _____ is equal to zero. The _____ is calculated as the mean square error: the sum of squared deviations about the mean, divided by the number of scores -1 degree of freedom.
a. Variance11
b. 15 theorem
c. Undefined
d. Undefined

42. <U>A <U>vertical line </U>goes up and down or from North to South.</U>
a. Vertical line11
b. 15 theorem
c. Undefined
d. Undefined

43. The _____ or central tendency of a list of n numbers. All the values are added together and then divided by the number of values. It is also call the mean..
a. Average11
b. ACTRAN
c. Undefined
d. Undefined

44. _____ is the result of assigning numbers to objects to abstractly represent the objects or characteristics of the objects.

a. Measurement11
c. Undefined
b. 15 theorem
d. Undefined

45. A <U>line segment </U>is a piece of a line. The _____ has definite length and is named by the two endpoints.
    a. 15 theorem
    b. Line segment11
    c. Undefined
    d. Undefined

46. The term _____ refers to a particular way in which observations will tend to pile up around a particular value rather than be spread evenly across a range of values. It is generally most applicable to continuous data and is intrinsically associated with parametric or inferential statistics. Graphically the _____ is best described by a bell-shaped curve. This curve is described in terms of the point at which its height is maximum, its mean, and how wide it is, its standard deviation.
    a. 15 theorem
    b. Normal distribution11
    c. Undefined
    d. Undefined

47. The _____ distribution is perhaps the most common of all distributions. The _____ curve is a property of the normal distribution.
    a. 15 theorem
    b. Bell-shaped11
    c. Undefined
    d. Undefined

48. _____ is the study of quantity, structure, space, and change. Historically, _____ developed from counting, calculation, measurement, and the study of the shapes and motions of physical objects, through the use of abstraction and deductive reasoning.
    a. 15 theorem
    b. Mathematics11
    c. Undefined
    d. Undefined

49. A <U>plane</U> is an undefined term. We can think of it as a series of lines having 2 dimensions, width and length.
    a. 15 theorem
    b. Plane11
    c. Undefined
    d. Undefined

50. _____ is a measure of how close an estimator is expected to be to the true value of a parameter.
    a. Precision11
    b. 15 theorem
    c. Undefined
    d. Undefined

51. _____ is the probability of a Type II error
    a. 15 theorem
    b. Beta11
    c. Undefined
    d. Undefined

52. For use in the analysis of the difference between two proportions. The _____ tests calculate a double-sided probability value for the relationship between two dichotomous variables, as found in a two by two table.
    a. Chi-square11
    b. 15 theorem
    c. Undefined
    d. Undefined

53. <U>Degrees</U> are used to measure the size of angles. A circle has 360 _____ in it.
    a. 15 theorem
    b. Degrees11
    c. Undefined
    d. Undefined

Chapter 12. Trigonometric Functions

1. An <U>angle</U> is composed of two rays that have a common endpoint, called the vertex. Each _____ is named by a lower case letter or by one point from each ray and the vertex inbetween. _____ a might be the same _____ as _____ ABC.
   a. ACTRAN
   b. Angle12
   c. Undefined
   d. Undefined

2. A <U>point </U>is an undefined term. We usually represent this by a dot, but a _____ actually has no dimension. A capital letter names any _____.
   a. 15 theorem
   b. Point12
   c. Undefined
   d. Undefined

3. A <U>ray</U> is part of a line that starts with an endpoint and goes on in one direction only. It is named by the endpoint and any other point on the _____.
   a. Ray12
   b. 15 theorem
   c. Undefined
   d. Undefined

4. A <U>plane</U> is an undefined term. We can think of it as a series of lines having 2 dimensions, width and length.
   a. 15 theorem
   b. Plane12
   c. Undefined
   d. Undefined

5. A <U>circle</U> is a series of points the same distance from a given point, called the center.
   a. Circle12
   b. 15 theorem
   c. Undefined
   d. Undefined

6. The _____ is the distance around a closed curve. _____ is a kind of perimeter.
   a. 15 theorem
   b. Circumference12
   c. Undefined
   d. Undefined

7. A piece of a circle is called an <U>arc.</U>
   a. Arc12
   b. ACTRAN
   c. Undefined
   d. Undefined

8. The <U>radius</U> of a circle is the distance from the center to the circle.
   a. 15 theorem
   b. Radius 12
   c. Undefined
   d. Undefined

9. <U>Degrees</U> are used to measure the size of angles. A circle has 360 _____ in it.
   a. 15 theorem
   b. Degrees12
   c. Undefined
   d. Undefined

10. A _____ is a well-defined collection of objects considered as a whole.
    a. Set12
    b. 15 theorem
    c. Undefined
    d. Undefined

11. _____ is a central branch of mathematics, developed from algebra and geometry, and built on two major complementary ideas, differential _____ and integral _____.

a. 15 theorem
c. Undefined
b. Calculus12
d. Undefined

12. Since the observations in most data distributions tend to cluster heavily about certain values, one logical measure of central tendency would be that value which occurs most frequently; and that value is referred to as the _____ or modal value. For a nominal scale of measurement, the _____ is the best indicator of central tendency.
    a. Mode12
    b. 15 theorem
    c. Undefined
    d. Undefined

13. _____ (from the Greek trigonon = three angles and metro = measure) is a branch of mathematics dealing with angles, triangles and trigonometric functions such as sine, cosine and tangent. It has some relationship to geometry, though there is disagreement on exactly what that relationship is; for some, _____ is just a subtopic of geometry.
    a. 15 theorem
    b. Trigonometry12
    c. Undefined
    d. Undefined

14. An _____ is any process or study, which results in the collection of data, the outcome of which is unknown. In statistics, the term is usually restricted to situations in which the researcher has control over some of the conditions under which the _____ takes place.
    a. ACTRAN
    b. Experiment12
    c. Undefined
    d. Undefined

15. _____ are intuitively defined as numbers that are in one-to-one correspondence with the points on an infinite line— the number line. The term "real number" is a retronym coined in response to "imaginary number" _____ may be rational or irrational; algebraic or transcendental; and positive, negative, or zero _____ measure continuous quantities. They may in theory be expressed by decimal fractions that have an infinite sequence of digits to the right of the decimal point; these are often (mis-)represented in the same form as 324.823211247... (where the three dots express that there would still be more digits to come, no matter how many more might be added at the end).
    a. 15 theorem
    b. Real numbers12
    c. Undefined
    d. Undefined

16. A number that does not change in value in a given situation is a _____.
    a. 15 theorem
    b. Constant12
    c. Undefined
    d. Undefined

17. The word _____ can have three meanings: In _____ theory, a _____ is an abstract object consisting of vertices (or nodes) and edges (or arcs) between pairs of vertices. The _____ of a function f : X ¨ Y is the set of all pairs (x,f(x)) The _____ of a relation, a generalisation of the _____ of a function.
    a. Graph12
    b. 15 theorem
    c. Undefined
    d. Undefined

18. _____ refer to any data source, whether individuals, physical or biological things, geographic locations, time periods, or events; that is, anything upon which observations can be made.
    a. ACTRAN
    b. Objects12
    c. Undefined
    d. Undefined

Chapter 12. Trigonometric Functions

19. A _____ is an undefined term. However, it is often thought of as a series of points. A _____ has one dimension - length. A _____ is either named by a lower case letter or by two points on the _____.
   a. Line12
   b. 15 theorem
   c. Undefined
   d. Undefined

20. The _____ refers to the amount of change in Y for a 1 unit change in X or is the ratio of the rise over the run; or in-other-words, the rate of change in the predicted value as a function of a change in the predictor variable.
   a. 15 theorem
   b. Slope12
   c. Undefined
   d. Undefined

21. The highest number in a list of values is called the <U>maximum.</U>
   a. Maximum12
   b. 15 theorem
   c. Undefined
   d. Undefined

22. The lowest number in a list of values is called the <U>minimum</U>.
   a. 15 theorem
   b. Minimum12
   c. Undefined
   d. Undefined

23. The _____ is often confused with the median. The Median is a statistic for the distribution whereas the _____ provides a statistic for an interval; it is the center of the interval; the arithmetic average of the upper and lower limits.
   a. 15 theorem
   b. Midpoint12
   c. Undefined
   d. Undefined

24. Addition (or summation) is one of the basic operations of arithmetic. In its simplest form, addition combines two numbers, the augend and addend, into a single number, the _____. Adding more numbers can be viewed as repeated addition. (Repeated addition of the number one is the most basic form of counting.) By extension, the addition of zero numbers, one number, or infinitely many numbers can be defined.
   a. 15 theorem
   b. Sum12
   c. Undefined
   d. Undefined

25. An _____ is an indication of the value of an unknown quantity based on observed data. More formally, an _____ is the particular value of an estimator that is obtained from a particular sample of data and used to indicate the value of a parameter.
   a. ACTRAN
   b. Estimate12
   c. Undefined
   d. Undefined

26. In a large distribution of data it is often easier to understand the data if it is grouped into intervals where each _____ can contain more than one data value. Distributions are often reduced to 10 to 20 intervals.
   a. ACTRAN
   b. Interval12
   c. Undefined
   d. Undefined

27. A _____ is a concrete example of an item or a specification against which all others may be measured. For example, there are "primary standards" for length, mass (see Kilogram standard), and other units of measure, kept by laboratories and standards organizations.

a. 15 theorem
c. Undefined
b. Standard12
d. Undefined

28. The _____ or central tendency of a list of n numbers. All the values are added together and then divided by the number of values. It is also call the mean..
   a. ACTRAN
   c. Undefined
   b. Average12
   d. Undefined

29. Any time one number is on the left side of another number on a number line, the first number is <U>less than </U>the second number. The symbol for this is <.
   a. 15 theorem
   c. Undefined
   b. Less than12
   d. Undefined

30. _____ describes the phenomenon where the values of distribution tend to move towards the summary statistic. For example, values in a distribution tend to cluster about the mean, and in a linear _____ equation, they tend to cluster about the linear _____ equation.
   a. Regression12
   c. Undefined
   b. 15 theorem
   d. Undefined

31. Statistical analysis, sometimes referred to simply as _____, is concerned with the definition and collection, organization, and interpretation of data according to well-defined procedures. The term itself, _____, is a defining characteristic of a sample, such as a sample mean, or sample standard deviation.
   a. Statistics12
   c. Undefined
   b. 15 theorem
   d. Undefined

32. The answer to subtraction is called the <U>difference</U>.
   a. Difference12
   c. Undefined
   b. 15 theorem
   d. Undefined

ANSWER KEY

Chapter 1

1. b	2. a	3. a	4. b	5. a	6. b	7. a	8. b	9. a	10. a
11. b	12. a	13. a	14. b	15. b	16. a	17. b	18. b	19. b	20. b
21. a	22. a	23. a	24. a	25. b	26. a	27. b	28. b	29. b	30. b
31. b	32. a	33. a	34. a	35. a	36. a	37. b	38. b	39. b	40. a
41. a	42. b	43. a	44. b	45. b	46. b	47. b	48. b	49. a	50. a
51. a	52. b	53. b	54. b	55. a	56. a	57. a	58. b	59. a	60. b
61. a	62. a	63. a	64. a	65. a	66. a	67. a	68. b	69. a	70. a
71. b	72. b	73. a	74. b	75. a	76. b	77. a	78. a	79. b	80. a
81. b	82. a	83. a	84. b	85. a	86. a	87. a	88. a	89. a	90. a
91. b	92. b	93. b	94. a	95. a	96. b	97. a	98. a	99. b	100. b
101. b	102. a	103. a	104. a	105. a	106. b	107. b	108. b	109. b	110. b
111. b	112. a	113. b	114. b	115. b	116. b	117. a	118. b	119. a	120. b
121. b	122. b	123. b	124. a	125. b	126. b	127. a			

Chapter 2

1. a	2. b	3. a	4. b	5. b	6. a	7. a	8. a	9. b	10. a
11. a	12. a	13. b	14. a	15. a	16. b	17. a	18. a	19. a	20. b
21. a	22. a	23. b	24. b	25. a	26. b	27. b	28. a	29. b	30. b
31. a	32. b	33. a	34. b	35. a	36. b	37. b	38. b	39. a	40. b
41. b	42. b	43. b	44. b	45. b	46. a	47. a	48. a	49. a	50. a
51. b	52. a	53. b	54. a	55. a	56. a	57. a	58. b	59. a	60. b
61. b	62. b	63. b	64. b	65. a	66. a	67. a	68. b	69. b	70. b
71. a	72. b	73. b	74. b	75. a	76. a	77. a	78. b	79. b	80. b
81. a	82. a	83. a	84. b	85. a	86. a	87. b	88. b	89. b	90. b
91. a	92. a	93. a	94. a	95. a	96. b	97. a	98. a	99. a	100. a
101. b	102. a	103. a	104. a	105. b	106. a	107. a	108. b	109. b	110. a
111. a	112. b	113. b	114. b	115. a	116. a	117. b	118. a	119. a	

Chapter 3

1. b	2. b	3. b	4. a	5. b	6. a	7. a	8. a	9. a	10. a
11. a	12. b	13. a	14. b	15. b	16. b	17. a	18. a	19. b	20. b
21. b	22. a	23. a	24. a	25. b	26. a	27. a	28. a	29. b	30. b
31. a	32. b	33. b	34. a	35. a	36. a	37. a	38. b	39. b	40. a
41. a	42. b	43. a	44. a	45. a	46. a	47. a	48. b	49. a	50. b
51. b	52. b	53. b	54. a	55. b	56. a	57. b	58. a	59. a	60. b
61. a	62. b	63. a	64. b	65. a	66. b	67. b	68. a	69. a	70. a
71. b	72. a	73. b	74. b	75. b	76. a	77. b	78. b	79. b	80. b
81. b	82. b	83. b	84. b	85. b	86. b	87. a	88. b	89. b	90. b
91. a	92. a	93. a	94. a	95. b	96. a	97. a	98. a	99. a	100. a
101. b	102. b	103. a	104. a	105. b	106. b	107. b	108. a	109. a	110. a
111. b	112. a	113. a	114. a	115. a	116. a	117. b	118. b	119. a	120. a
121. a	122. a	123. b	124. b	125. a	126. a	127. b	128. a		

Chapter 4

1. a	2. a	3. a	4. b	5. a	6. a	7. b	8. a	9. b	10. b
11. a	12. a	13. a	14. a	15. a	16. a	17. b	18. a	19. b	20. b
21. a	22. a	23. a	24. b	25. b	26. a	27. b	28. a	29. b	30. a
31. a	32. b	33. a	34. a	35. a	36. a	37. a	38. a	39. a	40. b
41. b	42. a	43. a	44. a	45. a	46. b	47. b	48. a	49. a	50. b
51. a	52. b	53. b	54. b	55. b	56. a	57. b	58. a	59. a	60. a
61. b	62. b	63. a	64. b	65. b	66. a	67. b	68. a	69. b	70. a
71. a	72. b	73. a	74. b	75. a	76. b	77. a	78. b	79. b	80. a
81. b	82. a	83. b	84. a	85. b	86. a	87. b	88. a	89. a	90. b
91. b	92. b	93. b	94. b	95. a	96. b	97. a	98. a	99. b	100. a
101. b	102. a	103. a	104. a	105. a	106. a	107. a	108. b	109. a	110. b
111. a	112. b	113. b	114. a	115. a	116. b	117. a	118. b	119. a	120. a
121. a	122. a	123. a	124. a	125. b	126. a	127. b	128. a	129. a	130. b
131. a	132. a	133. a							

Chapter 5

1. b	2. a	3. b	4. a	5. b	6. a	7. b	8. b	9. a	10. a
11. b	12. b	13. a	14. a	15. b	16. b	17. b	18. b	19. a	20. a
21. b	22. a	23. b	24. b	25. a	26. a	27. a	28. a	29. b	30. a
31. a	32. b	33. a	34. a	35. b	36. a	37. b	38. a	39. a	40. a
41. a	42. a	43. b	44. b	45. a	46. a	47. a	48. b	49. a	50. b
51. b	52. a	53. b	54. a	55. b	56. b	57. a	58. b	59. a	60. a
61. a	62. b	63. b	64. a	65. b	66. a	67. b	68. a	69. a	70. a
71. a	72. a	73. a	74. a	75. b	76. b	77. b	78. a	79. b	80. b
81. a	82. a	83. a	84. a	85. a	86. b	87. b	88. b	89. b	90. b
91. b	92. a	93. b	94. b	95. b	96. a	97. a	98. b	99. a	100. a
101. a	102. b	103. b	104. a	105. a	106. b	107. b	108. b	109. a	110. b
111. b	112. a	113. b							

ANSWER KEY

Chapter 6

1. b	2. a	3. a	4. b	5. a	6. b	7. b	8. b	9. b	10. a
11. b	12. a	13. b	14. a	15. b	16. a	17. a	18. b	19. b	20. a
21. a	22. a	23. a	24. a	25. b	26. a	27. a	28. b	29. a	30. a
31. b	32. b	33. a	34. a	35. a	36. a	37. b	38. a	39. a	40. b
41. b	42. b	43. a	44. b	45. a	46. a	47. a	48. b	49. b	50. a
51. a	52. a	53. a	54. b	55. a	56. b	57. a	58. a	59. b	60. b
61. b	62. b	63. b	64. a	65. a	66. b	67. a	68. a	69. b	70. b
71. b	72. b	73. b	74. b	75. a	76. a	77. b	78. a	79. a	80. a
81. b	82. a	83. b	84. a	85. b	86. a	87. b	88. a	89. b	90. b
91. b	92. a	93. b	94. a	95. a	96. a	97. b	98. a	99. a	100. b
101. a	102. b	103. a	104. b	105. a	106. b	107. a	108. b	109. b	110. a
111. b	112. a	113. b	114. b	115. a	116. b	117. a	118. a	119. b	120. a
121. a	122. a	123. a	124. a	125. b	126. b	127. a	128. b	129. a	130. b
131. b	132. b	133. b	134. a	135. b	136. b	137. a	138. a	139. b	140. b
141. a	142. b	143. a	144. b						

Chapter 7

1. a	2. b	3. a	4. b	5. b	6. b	7. b	8. b	9. b	10. a
11. b	12. b	13. b	14. a	15. b	16. b	17. b	18. a	19. b	20. b
21. a	22. a	23. a	24. b	25. b	26. a	27. b	28. a	29. a	30. b
31. a	32. b	33. a	34. a	35. a	36. b	37. b	38. b	39. a	40. b
41. b	42. a	43. a	44. a	45. a	46. a	47. a	48. b	49. b	50. a
51. a	52. a	53. a	54. b	55. b	56. b	57. a	58. b	59. a	60. b
61. a	62. b	63. b	64. b	65. a	66. a	67. a	68. a	69. a	70. a
71. a	72. a	73. a	74. a	75. b	76. b	77. a	78. a	79. a	80. a
81. b	82. a	83. a	84. a	85. a	86. b	87. b	88. b	89. a	90. a
91. b									

Chapter 8

1. a	2. b	3. a	4. a	5. a	6. b	7. b	8. b	9. a	10. a
11. b	12. a	13. b	14. a	15. b	16. b	17. b	18. b	19. a	20. b
21. a	22. a	23. a	24. a	25. b	26. a	27. b	28. b	29. b	30. a
31. b	32. a	33. b	34. a	35. a	36. b	37. a	38. b	39. a	40. b
41. a	42. b	43. a	44. b	45. b	46. a	47. b	48. b	49. b	50. a
51. a	52. b	53. a	54. b	55. a	56. a	57. a	58. b	59. b	60. b
61. b	62. a	63. b	64. b	65. a	66. b	67. b	68. a	69. a	70. b
71. a	72. a	73. a	74. b	75. b	76. a	77. a	78. a	79. a	80. b
81. b	82. b	83. a	84. a	85. b	86. b	87. a	88. b	89. a	90. a
91. a	92. b	93. b	94. a	95. b	96. b	97. a	98. a	99. a	100. a
101. b	102. b	103. a	104. b	105. b	106. b	107. b	108. b	109. b	110. a
111. a	112. b	113. a	114. b	115. a	116. b	117. a	118. b	119. a	120. a
121. a	122. b	123. b	124. a	125. a	126. a	127. a	128. b	129. a	130. b
131. a	132. a	133. b	134. b	135. b	136. a	137. a			

Chapter 9

1. b	2. b	3. a	4. b	5. a	6. a	7. a	8. b	9. b	10. a
11. b	12. a	13. a	14. b	15. b	16. b	17. b	18. a	19. a	20. a
21. b	22. a	23. a	24. b	25. a	26. a	27. b	28. b	29. a	30. b
31. b	32. b	33. a	34. a	35. a	36. b	37. a	38. b	39. a	40. b
41. a	42. b	43. a	44. a	45. a	46. a	47. b	48. a	49. a	50. b
51. b	52. b	53. b	54. a	55. a	56. b	57. b	58. a	59. a	60. a
61. b	62. a	63. b	64. b	65. b	66. b	67. b	68. b	69. a	70. a
71. a	72. b	73. b	74. a	75. b	76. b	77. b	78. b	79. b	80. a
81. b	82. a	83. a	84. a	85. a	86. a	87. b	88. a	89. a	90. a
91. a	92. a								

Chapter 10

1. a	2. b	3. a	4. a	5. b	6. a	7. a	8. a	9. b	10. a
11. b	12. a	13. b	14. b	15. a	16. a	17. a	18. a	19. b	20. b
21. a	22. b	23. a	24. a	25. b	26. a	27. a	28. a	29. a	30. b
31. b	32. b	33. a	34. a	35. b	36. b	37. a			

Chapter 11

1. b	2. b	3. a	4. a	5. a	6. b	7. a	8. b	9. a	10. b
11. a	12. b	13. b	14. b	15. a	16. a	17. a	18. a	19. b	20. b
21. b	22. b	23. a	24. b	25. b	26. b	27. a	28. a	29. b	30. b
31. a	32. a	33. a	34. b	35. a	36. b	37. b	38. b	39. b	40. a
41. a	42. a	43. a	44. a	45. b	46. b	47. b	48. b	49. b	50. a
51. b	52. a	53. b							

Chapter 12

1. b	2. b	3. a	4. b	5. a	6. b	7. a	8. b	9. b	10. a
11. b	12. a	13. b	14. b	15. b	16. b	17. a	18. b	19. a	20. b
21. a	22. b	23. b	24. b	25. b	26. b	27. b	28. b	29. b	30. a
31. a	32. a								

www.ingramcontent.com/pod-product-compliance
Lightning Source LLC
Chambersburg PA
CBHW082042230426
43670CB00016B/2753